Walking on Th

Walking on Thorns

The Call to Christian Obedience

Allan Boesak

William B. Eerdmans Publishing Company
Grand Rapids, Michigan

*I walk on thorns,
but firmly, as among flowers...*

From a poem
by Thich Nhat Hanh

© World Council of Churches, 150 route de Ferney,
1211 Geneva 20, Switzerland

First published 1984 by World Council of Churches as No. 22
in the Risk book series.

This American edition published 1984 through special arrangement
with WCC by Wm. B. Eerdmans Publishing Company,
255 Jefferson Ave. S.E., Grand Rapids, Mich. 49503

Library of Congress Cataloging in Publication Data

Boesak, Allan Aubrey, 1946-
Walking on thorns.

Previous ed.: Geneva, Switzerland: World Council of Churches, 1984.
Originally issued in series: The Risk book series; no. 22.
1. Reformed Church — Sermons. 2. Sermons, English —
South Africa. I. Title.
BX9426.B64W35 1984 252°.042 84-13782

ISBN 0-8028-0041-6 (pbk.)

Table of contents

FOR
JAN AND JOHANNA DE WAAL
JOHAN AND BETSIE RETIEF
DIRK AND LORRAINE MARAIS
BERTUS SCHREUDER

Obedience is better than sacrifice . . .
                                        1 Sam. 15:22

*I tell you this: there is no one who has given up home,
brothers and sisters, mother, father or children, or land,
for my sake and for the Gospel, who will not receive in
this age a hundred times as much — houses, brothers and
sisters, mothers and children, and land — and persecution
besides; and in the age to come eternal life.*

                          Mark 10:29,30

Preface

This little book is not a theological or philosophical treatise on Christian obedience. It contains seven sermons and one letter, all of them responses to actual situations which seek to give an account of faith and hope, and to discuss openly some of the realities we have come to understand through the demands of the gospel in South Africa today.

The idea of this book originated with my open letter to the Minister of Justice in South Africa, which was published in 1979. WCC Publications asked me to "expand the letter into a book". With my commitments in South Africa and elsewhere I could not then take up the proposal. In the summer of 1983 it was suggested that I put together some sermons in which I have dealt specifically with the theme of "obedience to God rather than to human beings". As it happens all of the sermons included in this book were preached during 1983, and they are all responses to specific situations which arose in that year.

To be obedient to God is an essential part of our Christian faith, and of the believer's calling. Our faith is constantly being tested. God does not ask of us a blind, unquestioning obedience, a kind of *Befehl ist Befehl* submissiveness. God does, however, ask of us a commitment, a trust, an obedience which is our response to God's love for and commitment to us. To obey God is to trust that God's promises will never change; it is to take the risk of faith, discovering the joy of the faithfulness of God. Obedience is growing in discipleship — understanding its pain and its cost. But it is also learning the joy of overcoming our fear of freedom, the joy of discovering what G.D. Cloete has called "heavenly solidarity".

These are all words, however. They must be given life and meaning. These sermons reflect that real life with which Christians are confronted. Committing them to paper now, I discover with some shock how personal a testimony some of them are. At first hesitant and somewhat embarrassed, I wondered whether this personal element would not prove to be a stumbling block for the reader who, after all, does not share with me, and the believing community with whom I worship, the events and the responses to them. But I have decided to let them stand unchanged. Obedience to God is ultimately not a cause for masses; it is a very personal decision. The events of which these sermons speak are now a matter of record. I had no choice but to be as frank and as honest as the situation demanded.

I have discovered that obedience to God in the situation in which so many South Africans live is not the result of a decision one makes once for all. It is a commitment that needs to be renewed every day. I have also discovered something else: the love God has for us, and which enables us to love God, liberates us for obedience, for the joy of freedom, the freedom to be freed from that fear of the cruel and violent people who know only the language of enslavement, intimidation and violence. It is not all a heavy, joyless burden, neither is it that sweet, suffocating social masochism that so many Christians have displayed over so many centuries. It is a joy that affirms life, to such an extent that those who really knew what they were talking about caught its spirit in a spiritual:

> ...And before I'll be a slave
> I'll be buried in my grave
> And go home to my Lord and be free!

But then they were slaves and understood why the struggle could also be a song, and why the crack of the whip and the sound of the gun could never drown out the promise of God.

This book is dedicated to some young white people in the NG Sendingkerk. They are close friends, people who have joined our struggle for justice, whose commitment and obedience spell such joy and hope. In the midst of the tragedy that is South Africa, they are a sign of God's kingdom; through their obedience they write different words on the pages of the life of our church.

A. B.

1. The LORD and the lords

As the LORD lives, said Micaiah, I will say only what the LORD tells me to say.

1 Kings 22:14

The king had already made up his mind: he was going to war. The war would be justified, for Ramoth-gilead was a city of some strategic importance which, according to Ahab, should belong to Israel under the peace treaty made three years ago at the end of a war from which Israel returned triumphant. Now, three years later, Ben-hadad, king of Aram, had not yet honoured his part of the bargain.

Besides, at the time Jehoshaphat, king of Judah, is visiting Ahab. Making rather clever use of the opportunity, Ahab puts the matter to his ministers who agree with his analysis. Probably at the same meeting Ahab consults the king of Judah who, besides being king of the sister kingdom in the south, is also brother-in-law to Ahab. What more fortuitous time than this?

Again Ahab gets what he wants, for Jehoshaphat, giving expression to the solid relations between Judah and Israel, replies: "What is mine is yours: myself, my people, my horses" (vs.4). The alliance is forged. Ahab is delighted. Politically and militarily all is in order — the king can go ahead.

Or so it seemed. But Jehoshaphat now introduces a completely new element into the discussion, at least an element of which there has been no mention up to now. "First let us seek counsel from the LORD," Jehoshaphat says.

Of course it was quite normal in the ancient East to consult an oracle before making an important decision. But in Israel one did not consult an oracle, one sought to learn the Word of Yahweh. It was an admission that one could not act alone. In Israel, the king was not simply king, he was king because Yahweh is King. The king knew that his authority was subject to the authority of the Lord. Obedience to God alone guaranteed the success of the king's rule.

It was to a king that Samuel proclaimed: "Obedience is better than sacrifice..." (1 Sam. 15:22). The prophet Jeremiah not only points to the sins of king Jehoiakim, but he also deals with the criteria of true and genuine kingship in Israel when he says:

> If your cedar is more splendid,
> does that prove you a king?
> Think of your father: he ate and drank,
> dealt justly and fairly; all went well with him.
> He dispensed justice to the lowly and the poor;
> did this not show he knew Me? says the LORD
>
> (Jer. 22:15,16)

Inasmuch as you knew the LORD, inasmuch as you obeyed the LORD, you were king. Jehoshaphat knew this, and therefore asked for "counsel from the LORD". Ahab, still in a state of euphoria after the victory at the meeting, had no objection.

Not that Ahab was "indifferent" towards religion and he did not care. He knew that a prophet would impart the Word of the Lord, and he also knew, like all the kings of Judah and Israel, just how troublesome a prophet could be. His whole life had been a confrontation with that irrepressible man of God, Elijah. "As soon as Ahab saw Elijah, he said to him, 'Is it you, you troubler of Israel?' (Elijah) replied: 'It is not I who have troubled Israel, but you and your family because you have deserted Yahweh and gone after the Baals'" (1 Kings 18:17,18).

Ahab was a king, and he wanted to act like a king. Of course he had his own policies and he wanted to execute them at all costs. He would not brook opposition nor the interference of prophets who knew nothing about politics or military strategy. Ahab was a king, and if he wanted more territory, he would take it, even if Naboth regarded his vineyard as a sacred heritage that he could not, would not, sell. He would take it, even if it involved corrupt practices, even murder. But Elijah the Teshbite would not let matters rest. Ahab would indeed *hear* the Word of the Lord: "Have you killed your man, and taken his land as well? ... Where dogs licked the blood of Naboth, there dogs shall lick your blood" (1 Kings 21:19).

Ahab was king, and he knew how to deal with a situation where, for diplomatic reasons, tolerance was called for. He would pursue a policy of tolerance in his relations with the Canaanites, the worshippers of Baal. It was a policy, Ahab thought, that guaranteed peace and prosperity, and especially unity within in times of external aggression. No, said Elijah. This land is Yahweh's, and he will not tolerate other gods. The choice was clear, for Ahab as well as for the people of Israel: "If the LORD is God, follow Him, but if Baal, follow him" (1 Kings 18:21). So it went, until all that was left was the threat of death uttered by Ahab's wife, Jezebel: "The gods do the same to me and more, unless by this time tomorrow I have taken your life as you took theirs" (1 Kings 19:2).

All this Ahab knew. He also knew that it would not do for him as king to be seen to completely disregard the religion of his own people, understanding as he did how fundamental that was to their lives. So Ahab surrounded himself with prophets — four hundred of them — who would impart to him the "counsel of the LORD". No, they were not prophets of Baal, of the kind confronted by Elijah on Mount Carmel only a short while ago. For all intents and purposes, they called themselves "prophets of Yahweh", who spoke, "moved by the Spirit of the LORD". They were the official prophets of the court, who prophesied precisely what the king expected them to say, prophets who never disturbed the peace and certainly not the "order" created by the king. They were the harmony men, who justified the king's every action and hence guaranteed a well-balanced relationship between church and state.

That has always been an exceedingly clever strategy. If religion is important to the people, if the pronouncements of the church can influence voting or the standing of the government, then do not eliminate the church, just own it. Don't do what the communists do — do better. That way you retain respectability, you remain a "Christian" government, and at the same time you rid yourself of the "turbulent priests" who interfere in politics, the troublesome prophets who constantly make a nuisance of themselves.

But a domesticated prophecy is not true prophecy. It is more like the second beast which rose out of the earth (Rev. 13), deceiving those who dwell on earth. It has two horns like a lamb, but it speaks like a dragon. The beast that looks so much like the lamb in fact seduces people to worship the beast from the sea which opens its mouth to utter blasphemies against God. While the Lamb calls for costly reconciliation, this beast preaches a false harmony. In the name of obedience it calls for blind submissiveness. With clever deceit, it fills the words of the gospel with meanings that do not belong to them. It invites us to dialogue, but it stops us from voicing the critical and crucial question: Whose interests are being served by this "reconciliation"? Who will benefit by it and who will be the victims? The true prophet of the Lord knows: this is not reconciliation; this is not the work of the Lamb but of the beast in the guise of a lamb.

Ahab's four hundred prophets are of one mind: the king must go to war, the king will overcome. Jehoshaphat is not impressed. Somehow — we are not told how — he is not convinced by the impressive unanimity of the four hundred. He asks: "Is there no other prophet of the LORD through whom we may seek guidance?" (vs. 7). The king has no choice: "Yes, there is one more... but I hate the man because he prophesies no good for me, only evil" (vs. 8). This is a strange way of putting it. It is almost as if the king is blaming Micaiah for his own failures. It is as if he believes that Micaiah has a strange power over destiny — an almost pagan belief that the prophet can influence the gods.

But of course Ahab knows that in Micaiah son of Imlah he has met someone who strongly reminds him of Elijah. Here is the same integrity, the same unshaking belief that he is called by God, the same conviction that he has heard the voice of the Lord in the stirrings of his conscience, in the cries of the poor and oppressed, and in holy rage against untruth and injustice. And the same total commitment to the service of Yahweh. Ahab also knew that, as long as he persisted in his policies, he will have prophets like Elijah and Micaiah ranged against him.

At this point Micaiah comes on the scene. We know nothing of him, except that at that point in Israel's history, he is the one who keeps alive the prophetic tradition. He is the true prophet in the tradition of Elijah, over against the prophets who speak not for Yahweh but for the king. As he listened to the well-meant advice of the king's official, he would have sensed what lay ahead. The king had the support of his ministers; Jehoshaphat had given his approval; the four hundred prophets had no doubt that the Lord would deliver Aram into the hands of the king. Zedekiah, a leading prophet, had even driven the point home by making for himself horns of iron and demonstrating by role play how the king would win.

The advice given to Micaiah was not altogether unsound. Logically, Micaiah could not expect Ahab to listen to him, when all others supported him and when the king himself had set his heart on the expedition. It would be foolish to challenge the four hundred prophets and the all-powerful king.

Not only was Micaiah so obviously an "agitator" in the eyes of the king (like Elijah before him), the four hundred had behind them the full and awesome power of the state. Being in a sense representatives of the state, neither they nor the king could afford to lose face in this matter. The prophets of the court were paid by the king — would they change their tune just because Micaiah felt differently? But Micaiah was clear in his own mind. He spoke words that span the ages, and even today they remain the fundamental touchstone for the relations between church and state: "As the LORD lives, I will say only what the LORD tells me to say."

These words point to the distinguishing mark of the true prophet: the constraint to speak Yahweh's truth whatever the risks, even against one's own interests; daring to do what is right, trusting only in the God whose voice you have heard.

They call to mind Dietrich Bonhoeffer's words: "We can no longer continue to exercise an attitude of restraint and justify it theologically as far as the actions of the state are concerned — such discretion is nothing but fear. 'Open your mouth for the dumb!' (Prov. 31:8) — who in the church today realizes that this is the least of the Bible's demands at such a time?" Or Oscar Romero saying to the Salvadoran government: "The church, defender of the rights of God, the law of God, and the dignity of each human being, cannot remain silent in the presence of such abominations... In the name of God, in the name of our tormented people who have suffered so much and whose laments cry out to heaven, I beseech you, I beg you, I *order* you in the name of God, *stop the repression*!"

They remind us of Martin Luther King defying the White House and challenging the whole political establishment in the United States over the issue of the war in Vietnam: "Somehow this madness must cease. We must stop now. I speak as a child of God and brother to the suffering poor of Vietnam... We *must* choose in this crucial moment of human history." Such is the voice of the true prophet, in the tradition of Elijah and Micaiah. "As the LORD lives, I will say only what the LORD tells me to say."

It is therefore all the more surprising that we find Micaiah in the king's presence repeating the empty phrases of the prophets in the king's employ. "Attack and win the day," he says, "the LORD will deliver it into your hands" (vs. 15). What does it mean? Some say that Micaiah is clearly making a fool of Ahab, playing with him, humiliating him in front of Jehoshaphat. That is possible. Others see in his words the masterly irony that the prophets of the Old Testament employed with such great style. That is also possible. But I would like to suggest something else. Is it not possible that Micaiah was serious when he said that, that his words were those of a man weary of struggle? As he arrives for his audience with the king, Zedekiah is enthusiastically demonstrating the victory of Ahab. Four hundred voices cheer him on. It is a deeply disturbing spectacle — such blatant pandering to the king's wishes under the guise of *prophecy*, in the name of Yahweh.

Micaiah is not unaware of the king's reputation. Ahab had rarely listened to the prophets of Yahweh, not even to a man like Elijah. He had allowed Naboth to be killed, he had allowed the prophets of Yahweh to be slaughtered. Micaiah's own fate may well be the same. Was it not said of Ahab that "never was a man who sold himself to do what is wrong in the eyes of Yahweh as Ahab did..." (1 Kings 21:25).

How much can a person take? The prophets of the Lord persecuted and killed. The king virtually helpless under the wicked influence of his wife Jezebel. The people scattered like sheep without a shepherd. A king who manipulates religion to suit his ideology, surrounding himself with paid prophets, so many of them, who will twist the word of Yahweh until it conforms to the will of the king. How long must one wait before Israel would learn to listen to the voice of Yahweh, turn away from the altars of death and choose life; before the lords of the earth will stop thinking of themselves as gods, challenging the Lord of heaven and earth? How long must one wait before the people learn to obey God's commandments, to "put away the evil of their deeds, (to) cease to do evil and learn to do right, (to) pursue justice, and champion the (cause of the) oppressed; (to) give the orphan his rights and plead the cause of the widow" (Isa. 1:16,17)? When will they learn that even with all their might and power they cannot mock the Living One?

How long must the prophets of the Lord call upon successive governments in South Africa to do justice and seek peace? And how much more blood must flow before they listen? How long must the prophets call for peace, pleading with the powers of the world to turn away from their mad pursuit of death and destruction?

When I discover (as I indeed discover more and more) that the things we struggle for today have been on the agenda of the churches for thirty, forty, fifty years, and with how much disdain, derision and hostility the true prophets who put them there have been treated, I am overcome with an indescribable weariness. Is it really worth it? No, I can understand Micaiah: "Attack and win the day..."

And yet, even as Micaiah speaks, he knows that the truth, Yahweh's truth, must come out. In the end, because he is the true prophet, he will say only what the Lord asks him to speak. This is a mood caught brilliantly by the Malaysian poet Cecil Rajendra, in one of his poems. He speaks for so many of us:

And yes, i too am
tired of protest
O to be done
with this madness
and like Khayyam
take to the wilderness
with a loaf of bread
a flask of wine
a book of verse
and a wild wild lass...

But now beneath
that nuclear
bough, Omar
there's no paradise
the bread crumbles
to radio-active pieces
the wine is toxic
the maiden
    leukemic;
a skeleton
screaming, not singing
in a wilderness
    of ash.[1]

And so he will speak, his will crumble under the onslaught of human pain and longing, under the hammer blows of truth and justice, in which he hears the voice of the Lord.

But the story gets more and more fascinating. It is not Micaiah who calls himself to order, it is the king who forces him to speak the truth. Does it appear strange? There is nothing strange about it. After all, deep down, Ahab knew the truth. He knew that the words of the mercenary prophets did not mean much. Those who buy people must know the actual worth of what they have bought. Imagine Beyers Naudé or Desmond Tutu telling the South African government that apartheid has God's approval. The government would be deeply suspicious — and rightly so.

---

[1] "Radiation and the Rubaiyat", from *Songs for the Unsung*, by Cecil Rajendra, WCC, Geneva, 1983.

Micaiah's words would have had the same effect on Ahab. He displays the curious contradiction we see so often: an unjust government needing deception yet not wanting to be deceived. And so Ahab adjures the prophet to tell him the Word of the Lord.

But he cannot take it. "I saw all Israel scattered on the mountains like sheep without a shepherd..." Micaiah is sent to prison. But there is someone else who finds the truth even more distasteful. Zedekiah, the prophet with the pair of horns, reacts angrily and strikes Micaiah in the face. In his commitment to the truth of Yahweh, Micaiah antagonizes the king; he antagonizes even more the prophets who deal in lies. Zedekiah strikes him because Micaiah exposes the "lying spirit" which is not prophecy but ideologized religiosity. He strikes him because, in the end, Zedekiah is only a creature, a tool of his master, and he can only respond like his master. As a response it is both reflection and justification. Zedekiah strikes Micaiah, Ahab sends him to prison.

That is the consequence. After Martin Luther King's Vietnam speech, the White House turned against him and he became *persona non grata* with President Johnson. Even more painful were the attacks upon him by fellow clergy and black brothers who had worked with him in the cause of civil rights. He could only say: "I know that justice is indivisible. Injustice anywhere is a threat to justice everywhere."

When Archbishop Romero took his stand, he was attacked by the hired theologians of the National Association of Private Enterprise, and his life was threatened. He could only say: "A bishop will die, but the church of God, which is the people, will never perish."

When Beyers Naudé opted for justice in South Africa, he was hated by his own people, dishonoured by his church, called a traitor by colleagues, and banned by the government. He could only say: "If the Word of God is not the fire that renews us, other fires shall devour us: if the Word of God is not the hammer that crushes rocks, other hammers shall destroy us. Listen, O people of God!"

And Desmond Tutu says to the Minister of Law and Order: "Mr Minister, we must remind you that you are not God. You are just a man. And one day your name shall merely be a faint scribble on the pages of history, while the name of Jesus Christ, the Lord of the church, shall live forever..."

2. At the risk of unity

*But when Cephas came to Antioch, I opposed him to his
face, because he was clearly in the wrong.*

Galatians 2:11

There is turmoil in the N.G. Mission Church (Dutch
Reformed Mission Church in South Africa). It is no longer
a far-off rumbling of disagreement; it is more like open
conflict. To the dismay of many, the disagreements are no
longer among ourselves, kept quietly within the circle, but
they have come into the open. The news media reverberate
with stories of how, at the highest level, we differ on fundamental points. "I feel so ashamed," one of us said the
other day. "Never before has there been so much tension in
our church, so much disunity. What will the world think?"

I have great sympathy for such people and I can understand their discomfort and confusion. For all the years of its
existence, the N.G. Mission Church has known "peace";
there was no disagreement or public argument. Now people
are being told that this peace was a false peace; that ideas so
long held sacred should be challenged, confronted and
changed. All of a sudden, the unity in our church is
threatened as never before.

This, of course, is not only true of the N.G. Mission
Church. Almost every church in this country knows the
agony of these tensions. The lines are being drawn. We are
beginning to discover that apartheid's greatest achievement
is not the racial division of the church, but the division in
our understanding of the gospel and its demands for South
Africa, the division of our interests, the division of the
people of God in terms of our faith and our ultimate
obedience to God. This is painful, but unavoidable.

But neither is this something new. Joshua finds himself
standing before the people: "If it does not please you to
worship the LORD, choose here and now whom you will
worship... but I and my family, we will worship the LORD"
(Josh. 24:15). Jesus drives the point home in even clearer
terms: "He who is not with me is against me, and he who
does not gather with me scatters" (Luke 11:23). Such
language calls for clear choices, it does not leave room for
compromise. From time to time, it seems necessary to re-

mind the Christian church of this, and every time such a reminder gives rise to painful conflicts and tensions.

Paul's letter to the Galatians is as good a reminder as any in the Bible. It is a letter with its own unique character, and it differs in so many respects from the other epistles Paul sent to the young Christian churches.

To begin with, in no other letter is Paul so tense, so upset, so angry with his Christian brothers and sisters. In all other letters, after the greeting and the blessing, he praises God for the young church and thanks God for its Christian witness. Not so in his letter to the church in Galatia. The greeting lacks the customary warmth: "From Paul, an apostle, not by human appointment or human commission..." This is not information simply for information's sake (the Galatians knew very well who Paul was); it sounds more like an angry reminder to people who should have known better than to doubt it.

Evident throughout the letter is Paul's sense of deep disappointment. "I am amazed — astonished, perplexed — to find you turning away so quickly from him who called you by grace..." (1:6). Shockwaves must have rippled through the gathering as the angry words were read to the whole church: "But if anyone, we or an angel from heaven, should preach a gospel at variance with the gospel which we have preached to you, let him be accursed!" (1:9). Paul talks of a "perversion" of the gospel; he makes no secret of his disagreement with Peter in spite of Peter's position of authority among the apostles. He denounces in stinging words those who mislead the people. They are "sham-Christians", "interlopers" who had "stolen in to spy upon the liberty we enjoy in the fellowship of Christ Jesus". They want to reduce the church to "slavery" once again, but Paul will not yield to them (2:4,5).

Members of the Galatian church are castigated for their "stupidity", their utter foolishness in allowing themselves to be "bewitched" (3:1). Do their past experiences mean nothing to them (3:4)? Do they now take Paul, who loves them, for an enemy — just because he speaks the truth (4:16)? And then, the note of personal disillusionment:

"You make me fear that all the pains I spent on you may prove to be labour lost" (4:11).

What is the cause of all this? Against what, and whom, is Paul raging so? Against the Judaizers, the commentaries say. Against the false doctrine of "the Law".

But what does it mean? Is it simply a "theological" matter, or is there more to it? I do not believe that "theological matters" are all that simple. Behind every theological argument one finds a complex of insights, a whole baggage of the past with its legacy of conflicts and interests.

The "law" under discussion here is the demand by certain Jewish Christians — the Judaizers — that gentile Christians should first be circumcized, and not only baptized, in order to be fully accepted as members of the new Christian church. Gentile Christians need *more* than just faith in Jesus Christ and acceptance of Jesus as the Messiah. They need what Jewish Christians already have and without which their faith will be incomplete — circumcision according to law.

Paul saw clearly, and with infinite sadness, what this really meant. The law was being used to legitimize an unevangelical, anti-gospel attitude. Behind the theological argument were people who thought themselves better than others, people who divided the church into classes, one more acceptable to God than others. They introduced other criteria for membership in the Christian church than faith in Jesus Christ.

Paul is fighting for the unity of the church, for the equality of all in the one church, for the acceptance of all by all. He is struggling for true solidarity among the members of the body of Christ, for genuine reconciliation, for the preservation of justice within the church, for the church as an example of love and justice and reconciliation in the world and as a sign of the kingdom of God. That is what is at stake here, and that is the reason for the conflict.

It is because he is fighting for the true unity of the church that he goes all out to unmask what passes for unity. So he will challenge not only the Judaizers, but also Peter who plays along with them. He knows that to maintain a false unity, the truth must remain crucified. That kind of unity can be maintained only at the cost of the dignity and the faith of the gentile Christians who cannot defend themselves. It can be maintained only at the cost of the gospel itself. Paul will not be satisfied with the kind of unity which militates against human dignity and the kind of peace which undermines human solidarity. Violate the integrity of the gospel and create an oppressed class within the one church in order to appease an apparently powerful group — that Paul cannot allow.

So Paul "opposed Cephas to his face". It was not the time for a private conversation, for cautious negotiation in order to reach a shallow compromise and present a united front to the church and the world. This was the time for open, public confrontation. The truth demanded it. Peter "was clearly in the wrong".

What seemed to have particularly incensed Paul was Peter's refusal to continue to eat with gentile Christians. That was a clear indication of how far Peter was willing to go to accommodate the Judaizers. They were both Jews; they understood the significance of eating with others, and of not eating with people.

To eat with someone is an honour, an offer of peace, trust, togetherness and forgiveness. It is to share with another not only the means of life, but life itself. It is an act of openness and vulnerability, solidarity and acceptance. It is not like a rich person providing food for the poor. What matters is the sitting down with the other. It is the affirmation of a relationship, a recognition of the shared humanity of the other. No wonder that the Pharisees were alarmed by Jesus' joyful eating with those they regarded as "sinners".

By refusing to eat with them, Peter took himself back to the old days, once again relegating gentile Christians to the ranks of *am ha'aretz*, those religiously and socially inferior. He considered himself above them, and cut them off from meaningful relationships and from the communion of the church. That is why Paul persistently reminds the gentile Christians: You are children of God; God is no respecter of persons, i.e. God is not impressed by human status or stature or class; you are free from the law. "For freedom, Christ has set us free!" Do not again become a slave to the law. Do not allow anyone to take away from you your dignity and freedom as the children of God. You have a place of honour in the church and in the world, for *Christ* has set you free!

Twice Paul tells them: "If we are in union with Christ circumcision makes no difference at all, nor does the want of it..." (5:6). What ultimately matters for the Gentiles, *and for the whole church*, is to understand this truth: "For you are all children of God through faith in Christ... There is neither Jew nor Greek, there is neither slave nor free, there is neither male nor female; for you are all one in Christ Jesus" (3:26,28).

This was what was at stake then; and this is what is at stake now, in our church, in this country. And this is the reason for all the tension, the disunity, the division in the church today. For almost a century, the N.G. Mission Church has played its expected role: to be an ethnic, separate church, giving tacit, at times open, support to the policies of apartheid, the evil whose very roots lie in the history of the Dutch Reformed Churches in South Africa. For almost a century we have lived under the ecclesiastical neo-colonialism of the white church, accepting its "missionaries", its apartheid teachings and its twisted theology, accepting its style and structures and its money. We never spoke out; when we spoke at all it was so clearly, so pitifully the *white* voice which spoke in and for this black church. The voices of our own prophets were drowned in a spate of threats, intimidation and derision. Many of us were bought — and effectively silenced. Still others were taught so well the language of the Pharaoh that they had no language left to speak for their enslaved people.

Then, in 1982, the N.G. Mission Church spoke. After a century of acquiescence, the Synod allowed itself to be moved by the Spirit of God and it spoke clearly: "We declare that apartheid is a sin, that the moral and theological justification of it makes a mockery of the gospel, and that its consistent disobedience to the Word of God is a theological heresy... We can do no other than with the deepest regret accuse the (white) Nederduitse Gereformeerde Kerk (NGK) of theological heresy and idolatry." We challenged the white church to recognize its guilt in creating and maintaining apartheid; we urged repentance and conversion. We asked that it should work out for itself "what the consequences of this confession of guilt mean in both church and state". The Synod did this "in love", in its role as prophet and priest towards the NGK in South Africa.

But the Synod went further. We accepted a Confession of Faith based on our belief that the struggle against apartheid is also a struggle *for* the integrity of the gospel and for the credibility of the Reformed tradition in South Africa and the world. The Confession of 1982 speaks of the unity of the church as both "gift" and "obligation"; it says that this unity must become visible and that "separation, enmity and hatred between people and groups is sin which Christ has already conquered". Therefore, "anything which threatens this unity has no place in the church *and must be resisted*". The church rejected "any doctrine which absolutizes either natural diversity or the sinful separation of people..." It rejected any doctrine which... "sanctions in the name of the gospel or of the will of God the forced separation of people on the grounds of race or colour..." And finally the Confession spoke of God as the One who wishes to bring justice and true peace to humankind. It affirmed that in a world full of injustice and enmity God is in a "special way the God of the destitute, the poor and the wronged and He calls His church to follow Him in this..."

So this is what is at stake in the witness of our church in South Africa today. Here is, I believe, the language of the gospel. Inevitably it has given rise to tensions and conflicts. The white church has rejected all this. For them apartheid still has divine sanction. They still support a government which is founded on apartheid.

Many in our church fear reprisals. The white church may withdraw even more of its funding. Ministers fear that they may not get their salaries. With the government we are no longer a "favourite" church in the black community; we are regarded as an enemy. Within the church itself there is a fierce battle between those who believe that the Synod has spoken the Word of God and those who believe that the

Synod should not have "meddled in politics", or that the judgment on the white church has been "too harsh". The 1982 Synod has suddenly exposed those who would like the church to continue to give support to the government and its plans for a new constitution. And, like elsewhere, it is becoming increasingly clear that the colour of the skin is no guarantee for being on the "right" or the "wrong" side of the issue. It is commitment and obedience that counts.

Many in the church are greatly disturbed. Our unity is threatened, they say: let's not fight among ourselves, let us leave others in peace. People are entitled to their opinions, they say: in the church we must talk, we must find one another, give one another room to differ... after all, we are in the church.

But that is exactly the problem! We *are* in the church! We are, as Kaj Munk of Denmark has said, in the temple of the holy God: "Others may have their allegiance to this and to that — we have our allegiance exclusively to the truth." What the N.G. Mission Church has discovered after all these years is the truth that apartheid is a lie and it should not be tolerated in the church and the life of our nation. We cannot any more accept that in the church we should convince each other not to convince each other. What the Confession of 1982 asks of the church, what millions of oppressed people are asking of the church in this country is that it participate in the struggle for human dignity and justice.

The church must make clear choices. How can we see the pain, the suffering, the blood, the cruelty of this system, and not make a choice for justice, peace and human freedom? If that choice means that we must openly oppose those who try to protect oppression and injustice through the use of gospel words like "peace", "reconciliation" and "unity", then so be it.

Not that the unity of the church is not a legitimate concern. But we are also concerned with the truth without which the church cannot live. We are concerned not so much about a common mind in the church as about the faithful obedience to the Lord of the church. If the unity of the church is not built upon the passion for truth, the desire for justice, the faithful obedience to the Lord whatever the cost, then it is not unity. Unity that is dictated by the powerful is not unity. Unity at the cost of the poor and the oppressed, at the cost of the integrity of the gospel, is not unity.

A long struggle lies ahead. Let us not revel in division, as if division in itself proves us in the right. Let us seek the true unity based on righteousness, justice, mercy and obedience to God. Let us continue to be inspired by the words of the Belgic Confession of 1566: "The faithful and elect shall be crowned with glory and honour; and the Son of God will confess their names before God his Father... all tears shall be wiped from their eyes; and their cause which is now condemned by many judges and magistrates as heretical and impious will then be known to be the cause of the Son of God..."

Jesus Christ is Lord. To the one and only God, Father, Son and Holy Spirit, be the honour and the glory for ever and ever.

3. Between the devil and the deep blue sea

Yahweh said to Moses, "Why do you cry to me? Tell the children of Israel to march on!"

Exodus 14:15

They were still walking on clouds as they marched towards the sea of reeds on their way to the promised land. Fresh in their minds was the memory of their liberation from slavery in Egypt. To many it must have seemed incredible: the mighty Pharaoh, king of Egypt, had no choice but let them go.

But their troubles were far from over. As they pitched camp beside the sea, Pharaoh was already regretting his capitulation: "What have we done, allowing Israel to leave our service?" He was, of course, thinking of his political prestige. Egypt was a strong nation at the time, a superpower. The Pharaoh was a god. He knew he was strong. To let these slaves go free, to succumb to the pressures put on Egypt by a man called Moses, to give in without even lifting a sword — that was humiliating.

And what will it do to Egypt's economy? No, this will never do. In the interest of national security he must rectify the situation. So it is that the Pharaoh decides to engage his troops in hot pursuit of the Israelites. It is always difficult for the oppressor to give up power!

Note how the writer of our story takes pains to describe the power, the awesome power of the Pharaoh. Six hundred picked chariots and all the other chariots of Egypt with officers over all of them. As he approached, Israel saw all of it: "the horses, the chariots of Pharaoh, his horsemen, his army..." (vs.9). Was all this necessary? Did he really need all this military power just to round up the unarmed slaves? Militarily speaking, no. There was no way in the world the Hebrew slaves could be a match for Egypt's military power. But the Pharaoh needed this show of power — desperately. It was the only response he knew — the language of threat, of intimidation, of destruction and death.

It is the age-old style of super-powers. Their weapons of death must protect them not only against the other, "the enemy", they must also protect themselves against their own fear. They surround themselves with armies and guns and tanks and missiles; and they hope that the world will not see their pitiful nakedness. The emperor's clothes.

Israel saw all this and thought this was the end. In front of them, the sea. Behind, the hordes of Pharaoh. They were caught. Between the devil and the deep blue sea. The panic was instant. Because it does not help much to complain to an invisible God, they directed their anger and fear towards Moses. "Were there no graves in Egypt", they ask with heavy sarcasm and bitterness, "that you must lead us out to die in the wilderness?" (vs. 11). We warned you to leave us alone! We were better off as slaves. At least we were alive. Rather a slave and alive than free and dead, they said. This must have surprised Moses (and God)! Egypt, the land of death, now becomes a land of promise and life. Egypt, the land of slavery, now turns into a land of freedom. But it is always like that: the fear in the hearts of the oppressor and the oppressed alike brings about strange reversals of reality.

But we should be able to understand the children of Israel, we black people. We know only too well the strange, deadly certainty there is in enslavement. You get to know the oppressor so well. You know when the Baas is in a good mood, good enough to let you get away with something. You understand his needs so well, so you call him "baas", you flatter him, you shuffle your feet, you demean yourself. You tell him how good he is although you don't believe that at all. You agree with him when he degrades your own people. You never challenge his authority. You agree with him that those who fight for justice are "communists", "agitators" who are out to spoil your good relationship. And in all of this you are sure of his reactions. As long as you keep to the fixed pattern of the slave-master relationship, you are safe. But freedom is different. The road to freedom bristles with contradictions and uncertainties; it is slippery with risk.

Besides, the power of the Pharaoh was something they had seen and known. They had firsthand experience of it. It was, in fact, much more real than the power of this invisible God who talked only to Moses. The fleshpots of Egypt (and the whips!) were much more real than the promises of a distant land "overflowing with milk and honey". They knew the Pharaoh much better than they knew this God who had left them in Egypt for four hundred and fifty years. No wonder they now tremble with fear.

How does Moses respond to this mounting mass anxiety? His words sound very much like our words in similar situations, the answers which we pastors are used to give, or are so often instructed to give: "Have no fear! Stand firm, and you will see what Yahweh will do to save you today... Yahweh will do the fighting for you: you have only to keep still" (vs. 13,14). In the light of the discussion between Moses and Yahweh (vs. 1-4) this was a good answer. After all, the Lord *did* promise that he would "win glory ... at the expense of Pharaoh and all his army". That could mean only one thing: God will help them out once again; the mighty hand of the Lord will stop Pharaoh and his armies and show Israel what it is to believe in the true God.

All the more strange, therefore, is Yahweh's answer to Moses in verse 15. "Why do you cry to me so? Tell the children of Israel to march on." Moses had not cried to God, but the people had. They had cried out to God and complained to Moses. God now seems to be speaking to Moses as the representative of the people. And God does not seem to be happy with the response of Moses. It calls on the people to stand still. It commends inaction. But the process of liberation calls not for passivity but for active participation. Freedom does not simply land on your plate, you have to work for it. Israel must now learn to take a measure of responsibility for the struggle. "Tell the children of Israel to march on!"

It is a strange command. Where should they go? Into the sea? There is nowhere else to go. To march on — that precisely is Israel's responsibility. It is to believe that this God, who has brought them out of slavery, who has walked with them through the desert, will now find a way to save them from the advancing armies of Egypt. It is to walk with God, finding a way where there is no way, to trust in God even though it seems that all possibilities have been blocked. They must have the faith that leads to obedience, even while Pharaoh's army is so ominously close.

This was the way of Israel. By faith Abraham obeyed when he was called to go out to a land which he was to receive as an inheritance; "and he went out, not knowing where he was to go" (Heb. 11:8). Israel must learn to obey the voice of Yahweh, the voice that offered life and called them away from death; the voice that spoke of freedom and called them away from slavery; the voice that spoke of love, justice and mercy, and called them away from inhumanity and oppression; the voice that spoke of the promise of wholeness and called them away from the pain of a shattered existence, estranged from one another and from the living God.

There was no blueprint, there were no certainties, no guarantees — "only the voice" (Deut. 4:12). And the voice called out to the children of Israel as they faced their ordeal, between the sea and the power of Egypt. It called for faith, for trust, for obedience. The choice for Israel was clear: with God, on foot, into the sea and the wilderness or, surrendering to Pharaoh, back to Egypt.

The government has seen fit to create a new constitution. Normally, this would not have mattered, since they are used to doing such things to us without our consent or participation. But this time it is different. This constitution makes provision for the limited participation of the so-called coloured and Indian people under white control and supervision. For the first time we shall have universal franchise. Not on an equal basis with the whites, mind you, but still we shall have the vote. Our political power will be severely curtailed, but we shall have a smell, a semblance, of it. We will have great economic benefits — the system is always willing to pay handsomely for cooperation. The "benefits" promised in the new system, the chance of belonging to the "white camp" in South Africa, the sheer weariness of the long struggle — these have enticed some of us to accept and support these new plans.

Many were therefore upset and disturbed when the churches, almost all of them, including our own, rejected these constitutional plans. Our reasons were clear:

— Racism, embedded in South African society, is once again written into the constitution.

— All the basic apartheid laws, those laws which are the very pillars of the system, those laws without which apartheid cannot survive — population registration, racial classification, group areas (residential apartheid), mixed marriages, to name but a few — remain untouched and unchanged.

— White minority rule and control over the economy remain entrenched, as apartheid remains entrenched.

— The homeland policy, which is surely the most objectionable and immoral aspect of the apartheid policies of the government, forms the basis of the exclusion of Africans, almost 80 per cent of South Africa's population, from the new deal. So the Africans will be driven even further into the wilderness of "homeland politics"; millions more will continue to lose their South African citizenship, and millions more will be forcibly removed from their homes into the desolation of these concentration camps called "resettlement areas".

So while these plans will mean something for those middle-class blacks who think that short-term economic gain is the highest good, they will not change the life of those who have no rights at all, who must languish in the poverty and destitution of the homelands, and who are forbidden by law to live together as families because they are black in "white" South Africa.

The church has no option but to reject these plans. And we reject them not only for the sake of political honesty and integrity, but for the sake of the church itself. Apartheid, in whatever form it comes, is contrary to the gospel of Jesus Christ. Apartheid is based on the premise that there is a basic irreconcilability between people who do not share the same ethnic, racial, or cultural background. The gospel tells us that in Jesus Christ reconciliation between and community among people are possible, however different their backgrounds. Apartheid exists only because of economic greed, cultural chauvinism and political oppression; it is maintained by both systemic and physical violence and it is based on a false sense of racial superiority. These are the very things which the gospel calls us to set aside. The gospel challenges us to accept the only identity that really matters, namely the identity of being a child of God through Jesus Christ, of being created in the image of the Living One, of being made a new creation through the life, death, and resurrection of Jesus Christ.

Furthermore, how can we speak of the unity of the Christian church, of the oneness of the body of Christ, when we accept at the same time that we should be divided politically on the basis of race, colour and ethnicity? How can the church witness to the justice and peace of the kingdom of God when we keep silent in the face of the ongoing injustice which apartheid, in the guise of the new constitution, represents?

The churches have always resisted apartheid. How can we change our stance now that some black people are going to be included into the system and will have to defend it? Surely the churches' resistance to apartheid has never simply been because black people thought it wrong. Our basis for fighting apartheid is the fact that it is a fundamental denial of everything the church stands for, a fundamental denial of all that is human and worthwhile in our society. We fight it because it is against the will of God for this country, and because in its claim to be based on biblical and Christian foundations apartheid is a blasphemous system, idolatrous and heretical.

So we must resist this modern Pharaoh from Pretoria, and we must learn to say "no". We must refuse to be intimidated by his might and power, and we must learn to say "no". I know the road ahead is full of uncertainties. The prospect is unclear. We would like to know exactly where we are going. We feel the pressures of our situation. We are afraid. Behind us is the Pharaoh and ahead of us only the sea and the wilderness. I hear the anxiety in the questions so many ask: all this talk about democracy and participation: is there anything more than words in it? Suppose we have a black government some day, will it be any better than the present white government? Is not the devil you know safer than the devil you don't know?

I know how so many feel. I have four little children who, I hope fervently, will have a better life in this country one day. I long for the day when they can live in a free and democratic South Africa, where racism will be a thing of the past, where people do not hate and fear one another. I pray to God that they will not become the victims of a struggle after the struggle, that they will not be devoured by a revolution that promised freedom and security. So many have died through the ruthlessness of a white government. So much blood has been shed already. If we have to wade through rivers of blood to gain our freedom, shall we ever be cleansed by the waters of love and understanding? If our call for liberation is distorted by the language of Egypt, shall we ever learn the tongue of the promised land?

We think of these things, and we become afraid. But our concern for the future must not deter us from doing what is right in the present. Amidst the voices of threat, intimidation and coercion; amidst the voices of temptation, cynicism and self-interest, there is that Voice again, exhorting us to do justice, to love mercy and to walk humbly with our God.

No, there is still no blueprint, there is still no guarantee, there are still no certainties — there is only the Voice, and the promise. We must take up the responsibility and we must march, believing, knowing that the One whose voice it is we hear will make a way. We must march, in faith, in trust, in obedience, and in the knowledge that God is with us, and God's power is greater than the power of the Pharaoh. The choice is clear: to go forward with God, through the sea and the wilderness, or to go back with Pharaoh and into slavery.

If God is for us, who can be against us?... For I am sure that neither death, nor life, nor angels, nor principalities, nor things present, nor things to come, nor powers, nor height, nor depth, nor anything else in all creation, will be able to separate us from the love of God in Christ Jesus our Lord (Rom. 8).

4. Into the fiery furnace

If our God, the one we serve, is able to save us from the burning fiery furnace and from your power, O King, he will save us; and even if he does not, then you must know, O King, that we will not worship your god, nor the statue that you have erected...

Was it not three men whom we threw bound into the fire?... Yet I see four men walking about in the fire, free and unharmed; and the fourth looks like a god.

Daniel 3:17,18; 24,25

This is a truly remarkable story. Israel is in exile in Babylon under King Nebuchadnezzar. Apparently the king has adopted a new strategy. He does not any longer treat all his captives as slaves. He has recruited some of the brightest among the young Jews to work for him. Not in lowly positions, but in positions of responsibility. The young Daniel and his friends, for instance, are not mere clerks in the lower ranks of the administration; they are men who bear political responsibility in the province of Babylon and at the court (Dan. 2:49).

There is, we notice much to our surprise, a certain cooperation with the oppressor. These talented young people have become administrators and governors, and they implement policy. Did they accept these posts because they could also *influence* policy in that utterly hopeless situation? Could they, by proving themselves to be better than the Babylonians, influence Nebuchadnezzar in his policies towards the Jews, and make it more bearable for their people in this strange land?

Whatever the reason, they cooperated, up to a point.

We may wonder, reading the Book of Daniel, how accurate the story is in a historical sense. But that is only a marginal issue. It is not the point of the story. Israel is in exile. The unthinkable has actually happened. The question now is how may God's people, now in strange land, sustain their hope and their faith under persecution and suffering?

For no matter how friendly an oppressor is, the oppressive power remains oppressive. Babylon could never be the promised land. How can the people, here in this situation, remain faithful to the God of Abraham, Isaac and Jacob? The Book of Daniel was meant to guide them through this difficult and trying time. By reminding them who they were: Israel, the people of the Living One. By reminding them of the truth that whatever the situation may be, however powerful the oppressors of this world are, however arrogant in their achievements — the Lord alone is King, and God will rise up and liberate the people from the hand of the powerful of this earth. The Book of Daniel speaks of the day of freedom, the day of the Son of Man, who will rule for ever. This message is proclaimed again and again in the book. It is proclaimed not only to the Israelites, but also to Nebuchadnezzar. And it is proclaimed not only through words but also through the prophetic deed.

The message comes through, vividly and clearly, in our story. It is proclaimed by the very people who have been trained at the court of Nebuchadnezzar, young men who have been elevated by him, from whom he would have expected less resistance and much more compliance. It is in the classic tradition of Moses, the slave who learned to read and write in the court of Pharaoh, now using his skill to organize his fellow-slaves to fight for their freedom.

Nebuchadnezzar made a statue of gold. Immense: ninety feet high and nine feet broad. Solid, immovable, indestructible. It was of incredible value. Was it a symbol of the power of the Babylonian empire? Or of the heights Nebuchadnezzar himself had reached? Was it how the king saw himself? Or was it a thank-offering to the god who brought him there? Or again, did the king and his god merge into one in this statue of gold, so that now the god was the king and the king was the god?

Of the significance of the image, there is nothing in the story. Perhaps the writer's silence is itself a comment. He has already described it; now he seems to be saying: Look at it: the staggering height of it, the breadth of it, the sheer wealth of it, the power it exudes; but it means... *nothing*. Not worth a single comment. This silence is perhaps the most telling commentary on the show of power on the part of Nebuchadnezzar, ruler of Babylon and all the world.

Israel often dismisses thus the pretentious gods other peoples set up and worship. With matchless sarcasm Jeremiah takes the myth of idols apart:

... the carved images of the nations are a sham, they are nothing but timber cut from the forest, worked with his chisel by a craftsman; he adorns them with silver and gold, fastening them on with hammer and nails so that they do not fall apart. They are like scarecrows in a cucumber field and they cannot speak, they have to be carried for they cannot walk. Do not be afraid of them, for they cannot do evil, and they have no power to do good... The nations are fools! Blockheads one and all, learning their nonsense from a log of wood...But the LORD is God in truth, a living God, an eternal king (Jer.10).

That last sentence from Jeremiah is the heart of the matter. Idols and false gods are not *harmless images*. They stand over against the Living God. They challenge the God of Israel. When Nebuchadnezzar sets up this idol, he takes the final step in his competition with Israel's God. To bow down before the idol means to acknowledge Nebuchadnezzar as God. This the three friends will not, cannot do. Now the lines are drawn, here all cooperation ends. The government which sets itself up over against the Living God oversteps the line. In its challenge to the Lord it loses all legitimacy, it deserves no loyalty, no obedience.

Shadrach, Meshach and Abednego could not forget the flaming words of the Torah: "You shall have no other gods before me..." Israel's God brooks no competition. The carved images of the nations cannot show forth God's love, God's mercy, and God's justice. They reflect the passing hopes and immediate fears of those who make them; they are creatures of time and place, "scarecrows in a cucumber field" set up to scare away the witless. But the God of Israel cannot be manipulated. "Uprightly he will defend the poorest, he will save the children of those in need, and crush their oppressors" (Ps.72:4). It was for this that God chose Israel "to do justice, and to love kindness, and to walk humbly with your God" (Micah 6:8). No image, not even the colossal one made of gold, can make such demands on people. The nations are fools, and so are the idols they make.

And so Nebuchadnezzar's challenge shall not go unchallenged. His order will not be obeyed. He is about to discover the limits of his power, not on the field of battle, but in the persistent, faithful obedience of three young men who refuse to be bought by his favours and submit to intimidation, even the threat of death. Nebuchadnezzar is about to discover that the old saying is not true — that when you have beaten a people in war, you have also taken captive their gods. Israel's God cannot be subdued.

Nebuchadnezzar is about to discover what Israel had known for ages, that Israel's true weapon in the struggle for the kingdom, the reign of God in this world, does not consist in arms that destroy and kill, it is true prophecy. That is why Elisha testifies, as Elijah, that symbol of all true prophecy, is taken up to heaven in the whirlwind: "My father! My father! Chariots of Israel and its chargers!" (2 Kings 2:12).

Not chariots and chargers, not guns and bullets, not Pershings and cruise missiles are the weapons of the church in the struggle for the kingdom of God, but the weapon of Israel: true prophecy, which is much less predicting the future than contradicting the present. And this is what the three young men are about to employ against the might of Nebuchadnezzar, the king of Babylon.

"These men, your majesty," comes in the report, "have taken no notice of your command, they do not serve your god, nor do they worship the golden statue that you have erected." "Furious with rage, Nebuchadnezzar sent for Shadrach, Meshach and Abednego..." (3:12,13).

Understandably. Their refusal is not so much a challenge to the religious unity the king sought to establish in his empire, as has been suggested. *That* was something all ancient (and modern) conquerors discovered quickly enough: the Jews cannot be religiously integrated. No, the king's rage stems from the fact that their refusal is a challenge to his political authority. When the king speaks, you obey. An order from the king is a divine command. No king worth his salt, with any understanding of the always fragile nature of his kingship, can afford to ignore such an act of open disobedience. The Jews may be allowed their religious eccentricities, as long as these do not interfere with political authority. But to challenge an order such as this is nothing short of a direct political challenge.

It is not clear whether the king called the three men to give them a second chance, to explain to them the political embarrassment they, as his protégés, were causing him, or whether his was simply another "kangaroo court". It is not clear whether he straightaway condemned them to the fiery furnace or whether he was wringing his hands in agonized indecision.

The writer of the book does not dwell on these issues. The internal turmoil of the executioner is not as important as the fact that the innocent continue to die. There are those who, in dealing with an atrocity, are inclined to call attention to the agony of the oppressor, as if one's powerlessness to eliminate a monster of one's own making must somehow guarantee for one a measure of innocence. As if the innocence constitutes the crime!

In the end, however, we must reckon with the endless arrogance of the powerful, the violent, humourless, merciless law-and-order people, whose self-confidence lies in their capacity to manipulate, intimidate and destroy — from ancient Eastern potentates to Roman Caesars to Soviet autocrats; from the Hitlers to the Amins, the Bothas, the Sebes, the Reagans of this world. The king says: "If you refuse to worship it, you must forthwith be thrown into the fiery furnace; *and where is the god who could save you from my power?*"

"My power". *That* is the bottom line. It is not religion, or the freedom of religion which is at stake here. It is power, it is the world as Nebuchadnezzar built it, knew it, wanted it. He could not conceive of that world giving way to the world as the Living God wants it, the world the three young Jews represented. And so the decision is made. The three young men should be executed.

Then follows one of the most remarkable sentences I know in the Bible: "If our God, the one we serve, is able to save us... he will... and even if he does not..." This comes as a shock. Isn't God all-powerful? Is not omnipotence the main attribute of God? Does it not mean that there is *nothing* God cannot do? Surely there must be some mistake here? In fact many translations render it differently. They read something like this: "If there is a God who is able to save us, then it is the God whom we worship..." Or: "Our God whom we worship, is able to save us..." That does sound more like it; it fits much better into the understanding we have become used to over so many years. But it is not what this text says. The Aramaic in which this part of Daniel is written leaves us no choice but to translate: "If our God, the one we serve, is able to save us..."

Here we stumble upon that strange, disturbing truth which the Bible does not try to conceal: the God whom we worship, the all-powerful God, is also a vulnerable God, a weak God. And it upsets us. Just as we are upset with Mark's candour about Jesus in Nazareth: "And he could do no mighty work there..." (Mark 6:5). We are shaken by the frankness of the statement. It seems as if there is no certainty at all. The risk of faith remains a risk.

Here is faith, but not in a God who, come what may, will deliver us. Here is faith in a God who may not at all be able to deliver us. Here it would seem that the power of Nebuchadnezzar can limit the power of God, that in the face of his power, God becomes powerless. "*If* our God... is able to save us..."

Why is this so profoundly disturbing? Is it not because we are conditioned by the concept of an all-powerful God, a concept which (and this is the problem) is born out of our own idea of earthly power — an almighty God who can match, and outdo, word for word, deed for deed, the powerful of the earth who persecute God's children, a powerful God who *always*, in the end, miraculously steps in to save, a sort of superman? We are enthralled by James Bond and Superman not so much because they provide such "marvellous, entertaining escapism" as because they reaffirm such deep religious needs.

"And even if he does not, then you must know, O King, that we will not serve your god or worship the statue you have erected." This, it seems to me, is faith. This is true obedience. To obey God when there is no way out of the fiery ordeal. To obey even when there is no certainty that God will provide an escape by miraculously stepping in at the last minute.

But it is disturbing. It raises inevitable questions. Do we believe and do we obey because we hope that the almighty

God will always provide an escape? Does this all-powerful God have to be the guarantee of our faith and our obedience? Do we talk about the "risk of faith" only because we know that we believe in an all-powerful God, so that this "risk" is really no risk at all? And is this the reason why we are in general so hesitant, apathetic, afraid?

For the question-marks of history remain. Dietrich Bonhoeffer's Christian convictions brought him to resist Hitler. Yet he dies, even as the guns outside Berlin announce that Hitler's moment of unholy glory is finally over. Was Hitler more powerful than God? Is God powerless against the South African government? And yet Steve Biko dies, naked, horribly, at the hands of those who also profess to be Christian. Martin Luther King could have given the world so much more. He taught us love, obedience, courage. And yet this apostle of love and non-violence is killed by the violence he himself refused to employ. Is God less powerful than the forces of evil? Archbishop Oscar Romero dies with the chalice of holy communion in his hands. Was God not powerful enough to stop the death of such a man? The fire rages on, the flames leaping up in their eagerness to devour. And dare we believe, and obey?

"They were then bound... and thrown into the burning, fiery furnace." No miracle happens. It is over. Or is it? The king springs to his feet in amazement: "I can see four men walking freely in the heart of the fire..." (vs.25) Here lies the wonder of it all. God does not extinguish the fire but does much more: God moves into the fiery furnace with Shadrach, Meshach and Abednego. And they discover not only the meaning of true obedience, they also discover the joy of what has been called heavenly solidarity, which follows human obedience.

For the joy of the obedient child of God lies not in the fact that the risk is eliminated or the trial set aside, so that the act of obedience would no longer be necessary. No, it lies in the discovery that this God will suffer with you. The God whom Shadrach, Meshach and Abednego served is the God who was afflicted in all their afflictions (Isa. 63:9), and the angel of God's presence saved them. In the apocryphal addition to this story we are told that God's presence "fanned in to them, in the heart of the fiery furnace, a coolness such as wind and dew will bring..."

At a difficult and trying time I received a call from one of the members of our congregation. "It may not mean much," she said, "but I wanted to let you know that we are praying for you. Don't give up the struggle for what is right and just." Then she gave me a text from Ps. 91 to remember: "Because he cleaves to me in love I will deliver him; I will protect him because he knows my name..." As I stood there, feeling the strength and joy of such love, my eyes became blurred but my vision cleared, and I understood something of what it meant to have God with me in the fiery furnace.

We are afraid, we turn away from genuine obedience, we succumb to the pressures and intimidation of the powerful because God does not seem to strike down our executioners. The fiery furnace keeps threatening. Does it mean that God is weak? Is God weak because the divine response is not commensurate with human expectations?

God does not respond to Nebuchadnezzar in terms of Nebuchadnezzar's power. True. But then God's power is a totally different kind of power. God's "weakness" is not the powerlessness which is the opposite of power; it is an alternative kind of power. It is not weakness but *strength* that enables God to become one with us, even in our suffering and pain, and through being present to deliver us. To have a powerful God is wonderful, and our God is powerful. But to have a powerful God who "...emptied himself, taking the form of a servant...and became obedient unto death, even death on a cross" (Phil. 2:6-8) — that is grace and power for us.

It is this truth which the slaves of America discovered a long time ago and immortalized in the joyful words of a spiritual:

I have heard the voice of Jesus
and he promised never to leave me alone.
Never alone, no, never alone
He promised never to leave me alone.

The presence of God in trial and suffering, in the fiery furnace — this is divine solidarity. God's presence in the midst of pain and terror and the threat of death is not a presence that sanctions or placates. It is not opium for a suffering, oppressed people. It is not a legitimizing presence but a protesting presence. God goes with us into the fiery furnace, and creates a coolness such as wind and dew will bring.

And the world is amazed.

5. The Reuben option

> But when Reuben heard it, he delivered him out of their hands, saying: "Let us not take his life." And Reuben said to them: "Shed no blood; cast him into this pit here in the wilderness, but lay no hand upon him" — that he might rescue him out of their hand, to restore him to his father.
>
> Genesis 37:21,22

Joseph was the favourite son of his father. He was, of course, the son of Rachel, Jacob's first and real love. He was also the son of his father's old age — not simply the son Rachel bore to him when he was already well on in years, but also the son who was such a comfort to him in his old age.

Joseph is special. All God's promises to Abraham and all the hopes of Jacob are now centred in this favourite son. His name means "add" — he is added, by the love and grace of God, a special gift from God which reshapes everything.

Joseph's birth marks a decisive change in the life of Israel. This son is a sign to Jacob that the promise of God still works in his life and in his body. Joseph is the last, because little Benjamin does not feature here. Once again we see the wonderful inversion of life's order by Yahweh: the last becomes first. That is why Joseph receives from his father the multicoloured robe with the long sleeves, a sure sign that he is the chosen one, the "crown prince", the one who will lead the family.

Spoiled, too young to do hard work, Joseph easily becomes a tattletale. Able to get away with things the older brothers are not permitted, his actions elicit the chagrin of his brothers. But that clearly is not the main reason for their hatred and jealousy. The real reason is something else: Joseph dreams.

Joseph dreams, but in a real sense he is only the bearer of dreams. The dream is Yahweh's dream, for Israel, for the world. The dream is a vision of history being inverted, undermined, changed against all odds. Joseph's dream is a power which neither tradition nor force can resist. It is a dream in which the impossible happens, the weak becomes strong, the lowly is raised up, the powerless is crowned with glory.

The brothers hated him because the dream threatened them. "They hated him, and could not speak peaceably with him" (vs.4), a wonderfully loaded phrase. Not only were they "unkind" to him, they could never be *at peace* with him; he was no longer a brother, he became an enemy. The decision to kill him does not really surprise us, it is almost inevitable.

Jacob provides the opportunity by sending Joseph to his brothers as they were tending flock near Shechem. "Here comes the dreamer," they say. Literally, here comes the lord, the master of dreams. A "master of dreams" is one who uses dreams to manipulate and intimidate others. The dreams now are not really visions, they are an instrument with which to gain control over others. As a sorcerer would use his powers, preying on superstition and the deep-seated fears of his victim, so Joseph is accused of using his dreams to intimidate and to control both his father and his brothers. They do not see his gift as a gift of God; for them it is not God's way of revealing the divine purposes for the chosen family and for the whole created world. They can only see Joseph's dream as a threat to the present order in which they have the upper hand. It is no longer a petty family quarrel — it is a life and death struggle. They simply *had* to kill him.

Reuben is not with his brothers in their strident demand that Joseph be put to death. He sounds so reasonable, so responsible — especially responsible. He emerges as Joseph's protector, saving him from certain death so that he could bring him back to Jacob.

Or so it seems. In reality, Reuben's role is much more ambiguous. He is the eldest, and therefore has special responsibilities. He is the one who must protect the family when the father is not present. He must also protect the family name and honour.

But Reuben's record is not all that clean. He seems to have shown little of the older brother's sense of responsibility as the tension builds up between Joseph and his brothers, and, by implication, the tension between the brothers and the father. There is no reconciling word, no attempt to mend the relations. No sign that he was trying to restrain his brothers as the grumbling grew more and more ominous. Even worse, Reuben has long since lost the confidence of his father, and his rightful place as the eldest, by sleeping with Bilha, Jacob's concubine.

What made him commit this grievous sin, "shaming his father's bed"? Was it a calculated move to secure for himself the headship of the clan, a strategy that was not uncommon in the ancient East where the successor to the throne inherited also the harem? This act of Reuben's was probably more than passing passion; it was perhaps in the nature of the declaration of a take-over. For Reuben, Israel was no longer "father"; he was an old man, a rival who stood in his way to the top. With infinite sensitivity, in words pregnant with tragedy, the narrator simply notes: "...and Israel heard of it" (Gen. 35:22).

So now Reuben engages in deception to save his brother. More for his own sake than Joseph's. Is it meant to restore Joseph to his father, or to restore Israel's faith in his eldest son? "Let us not spill blood," Reuben says, "let us throw him into the pit..." He appears to speculate on the effect of the superstitious fear over the spilling of blood, something we find expressed in Genesis 9:6 — as if murder would go unpunished as long as no blood is spilled.

But Reuben dares not choose openly for Joseph, he does not want to give up his popularity with his brothers now, and their support later, for his headship of the clan. So he sacrifices on two altars, as it were. He desperately wants to regain his father's favour, but he cannot risk alienation from his brothers. He knows what is right, he knows what he must do, but his hidden interests weigh too heavily on the other side. So Reuben opts for the feeble role of the "responsible" brother; his aim is to keep both sides happy, to do enough to salve his own conscience, but not enough to save the life of his brother.

Joseph is sold into slavery, and slavery is only a different kind of death. The fact that Joseph, many years later, can say that "it was not you who sent me here, but God" (45:8) does not alter this situation. Neither Joseph nor Reuben could have known this. The grace of God which turns evil into good can never be an excuse for our continued sinfulness. Reuben is not presented here as an evil man. He is not a murderer. No, he is presented as concerned and responsible. As Walter Brueggemann says: "Reuben is presented as responsible, but cowardly, and the killers of the dream will not be restrained by a responsible coward."

This, I think, is the agony of the church: we know what we should be doing, but we lack the courage to do it. We feel we ought to do it and we cannot. We are afraid to make choices, so we are constantly on the look-out for compromises. We are paralyzed by the need to be all things to all people, to be a church where all feel welcome all the time, and so we sacrifice on both altars. We stand accused by a history of compromises always made for the sake of survival.

We have justified slavery, violence and war; we have sanctified racism and split our churches on the issue of the preservation of white supremacy. We have discriminated against women and kept them servile whilst we hid our fear of them behind claims of "masculinity" and sanctimonious talk about Adam and Eve. We have grown rich and fat and powerful through the exploitation of the poor, which we deplored but never really tried to stop. All in the name of Jesus Christ and his gospel. Now this same gospel speaks to us, and we can no longer escape its demands. It calls us to love and justice and obedience. We would like to fulfill that calling, but we do not want to risk too much. The Reuben option.

The Reuben option: Take a stand, but always cover yourself. The problem cannot be ignored, so let us do something about it, but always in such a way that it does not hurt us too much. Take a stand; use the right words in the resolutions taken by the synod and the general assembly, but also make sure that you build into those resolutions all the necessary safeguards — just in case. Don't antagonize people too much, especially those in the church who have money. Opt for peace, but don't confuse that with justice.

The Reuben option: How often do we face it in my own country and in my own church! We know we have to say that we are against injustice, racism and apartheid. We know that we must work for the kingdom of God, work in such a way that people's humanity will be restored, but we are afraid to join the struggle for liberation, to participate actively in that struggle. The risks are too many. Let us pass resolutions against apartheid, but let us frame them in such a way that we can defend ourselves when the white church threatens to withdraw its money.

The Reuben option: Opt for justice, work against racism, but in such a way that we will not cause too much tension in the church. Was that not how the world church functioned for many years? Think of all the controversy and the conflict over the World Council of Churches' Programme to Combat Racism. We came close to losing our unity on that issue, we almost jeopardized our whole Christian witness on it. So the churches went through agonizing times. How do we support the PCR and yet do it in such a way that no one (especially those conservatives who hold the purse strings) can accuse us of giving money to "terrorists"? To our shock we discover that we have to choose constantly between the interests of those who can afford to make television programmes "exposing" the PCR and the interests of the oppressed, the poor and the weak, the victims of exploitation and racism, who also happen to be our brothers and sisters in the Lord.

The Reuben option: Have a programme for hungry children, collect millions and spend them on the poor. "Give and feel good!" is the legend on a poster from one charitable organization, with a picture of a little black child, arms grotesquely thin, protruding stomach, tears rolling down the cheeks. Yes, indeed. But to use all our energy, our resources, our ingenuity, to work honestly and openly to change an economic system that by its very nature cannot and will not give the poor a chance to become fully human? That we cannot do, because then we become "involved", and we have to look with new eyes at the systems on which our budgets are based.

The Reuben option: We face that ourselves. I know that we are called to serve God's kingdom in terms of peace and justice and human dignity. But how difficult it is when this call stands in the way of our ambition! When we live under the threat of death every day, when we are always only one step away from being "picked up", when they tell us that our name is "on the list" because we are a danger to "Christian civilization" —how difficult it is then to make that choice! And I have discovered that the choice for commitment and obedience is not made once for all. It is a choice that has to be made every day.

The Reuben option. And so we invent little excuses and we dress them up as theological arguments about church and politics, violence and non-violence, personal and public morality and, above all, responsibility. We call ourselves evangelical and ecumenical and fight one another; in the meantime the poor continue to be exploited, the weak continue to be trampled upon and the innocent continue to die. And we *know* we are being unworthy of the gospel.

"It is so difficult!" someone will say. Indeed it is. We are not "merely" human, we are *human*! But we are not the church of Reuben, we are the church of Jesus Christ. Are we not therefore able to do more than we think we can? Are we not those who will move mountains if we have faith "like a mustard seed"? Are we not those called by Jesus Christ to do his work in the world? Are we not those saved by him, and has he not made known to us "the mystery of his will" (Eph. 1:9)?

I know we sometimes say: the situation is more complex than we think; we have to be careful, because the most important thing is the survival of the church. I would, however, like to submit to you that the survival of the church is none of our business. It is God's business. We must simply learn to trust God to take care of it. Why should we be so worried about the survival of the church? Maybe because for us that often means: don't antagonize those who give the most money. Sometimes it means: don't antagonize the powers that be. But do we really believe that any earthly power can destroy the church of Jesus Christ? No, the survival of the church is *not* our main problem. Our main problem lies within ourselves, and with our difficulty to be faithful and to be obedient, to love justice and mercy and to walk humbly with our Lord.

Kaj Munk was a pastor of the church in Denmark. He became the spiritual force behind the Danish resistance to

Hitler at the time of the Nazi occupation. In January 1944, they took him away one night and shot him like a dog in the field, but his life and death continued to inspire the Danes in their struggle for freedom. To me, Kaj Munk is one of the great men in the recent history of the Christian church. He reminded his fellow pastors of what they needed in a world where the choices were becoming more stark, more painful, more unavoidable day by day. "What is therefore the task of the preacher today? Shall I answer: faith, hope and love? That sounds beautiful. But I would rather say: courage. No, even that is not challenging enough to be the *whole* truth... Our task today is recklessness... For what we as (church) lack is most assuredly not psychology or literature. We lack a holy rage..."

A holy rage. The recklessness which comes from the knowledge of God and humanity. The ability to rage when justice lies prostrate on the streets and when the lie rages across the face of the earth. A holy anger about things that are wrong in the world. To rage against the ravaging of God's earth and the destruction of God's world. To rage when little children must die of hunger while the tables of the rich are sagging with food. To rage at the senseless killing of so many and against the madness of militarism. To rage at the lie that calls the threat of death and the strategy of destruction "peace". To rage against the complacency of so many in the church who fail to see that we shall live only by the truth, and that our fear will be the death of us all... To restlessly seek that recklessness that will challenge, and to seek to change human history until it conforms to the norms of the kingdom of God.

And remember, says Kaj Munk, "the signs of the Christian church have always been the lion, the lamb, the dove and the fish. But *never* the chameleon." And remember too: the church is the chosen people of God.

But the chosen shall be known by their choices.

6. ...And even his own life...

If anyone comes to me and does not hate his father and mother, wife and children, brothers and sisters, even his own life, he cannot be my disciple.

Luke 14:26

Luke 14:25-35 is the culmination of a series of confrontations between Jesus and the Pharisees and the lawyers, a conflict which begins in chapter 11. All the time Jesus was challenging the Pharisees and the lawyers, the leaders and the scribes, the powerful in the synagogue and in society, overturning their values, exposing their hypocrisy and undermining their authority. He castigated them for their fanatic adherence to the letter of the law while they denied the very life of the Torah: love and justice.

We can feel the tensions building up as we read on. Jesus keeps on digging deeper; he keeps on narrowing the focus. He keeps on sharpening the conflict as he relentlessly peels away the side issues and forces his listeners to face the heart of the matter.

He not only challenges the authority of the rulers of the synagogue by healing the sick on the Sabbath, he also challenges all worldly authority, all political authority, and calls for the acknowledgment of a higher loyalty and a higher obedience. He not only reminds his followers of the One whose power extends beyond the death of the body and therefore is the true one to fear (12:4,5), he also reminds them of their witness in the world, the fearlessness which is needed for that witness and the temptation to disown him before the world.

He is disturbingly honest about his mission and its consequences. He declares that he did not come to bring a superficial kind of peace but fire instead. He is uncompromising in his demands and the lines are clearly drawn: "He who is not for me is against me..." (11:23). But he did not expect of others that which he was not willing to take upon himself. The fire was burning inside him and he knew that he had to be obedient, even though it would mean that he would not escape the lot of the true prophet (13:31-35). Of course, the clash is unavoidable. Here is the parting of the ways.

Jesus' radical call for conversion and repentance is exactly what these people are not ready to submit to. Besides, it has become clearer now: the choice the Messiah makes of the weak, the despised and the poor alienates the rich, the powerful and the privileged. What happens then must happen: Jesus loses them. What is summarized in a single sentence in the story of the rich young ruler is spelt out here three times in a row.

But Luke continues to unfold his story. There are more surprises in store. Unpleasant ones. When the rich and the powerful, the pompous and the self-assured (who are of course no longer so sure of themselves) leave, the conflict, surprisingly, disturbingly, is not over. "Great crowds" continue to accompany Jesus. Presumably these are the people who have not broken away, the people who apparently want to remain with Jesus because they think they have passed the test. They are not the rich who cannot bear to leave their possessions. These are the people who are ready to face the challenges of discipleship. Or so they think.

Now Jesus turns to them. He does not address "the crowds", he speaks to the individual: "If anyone (of you) comes to me..." Here is an appeal to the personal responsibility each one of us has to make a personal decision. Here is the end of the safety that is in numbers, of the comfort of being part of a crowd. That feeling of security melts and disappears in the scorching flame of this personal demand: "If anyone comes to me and does not hate his father and mother, wife and children, brothers and sisters, even his own life, he cannot be my disciple."

It is almost as if Jesus does not *want* anybody to follow him. He invites them to think twice, to be clear about the consequences of such a step, to look before they leap. He appeals to their reason, indeed to their caution: "Would anyone of you think of building a tower without first sitting down and calculating the cost? ..." Here is no sign of the ecstatic, romantic "overcome-by-the-Spirit" emotionality that is the hallmark of so much empty TV-religiosity, where acceptance of Jesus is part of the glitter of pious entertainment, and where discipleship is reduced to the dazzling flow of words and the even more dazzling flow of dollars. And

meanwhile the gilded cross in the corner becomes a grotesquely grinning golden calf.

No, there is no sign of that here. Jesus is almost saying: You have been warned. Don't start something you
cannot finish. Think! And so the soberness of this warning strips away all our pretensions and leaves us with the
naked realities of decision: to hate father, mother, wife
and children, brothers and sisters, and even your own
life...

At this point I can sense your discomfort and uneasiness.
I think I know exactly how you feel. I have been in the
ministry for fifteen years now, and not once have I preached
on this text. To tell you the truth, I was too scared to do so.
I did not know how to do it. These words are too harsh, too
uncompromising, too demanding. They did not fit in with
my own ideas of what discipleship was and I had the feeling
that my own ideas of discipleship were just a little bit too
easy, too well-defined, too comfortable. I was not ready to
deal with words like these, and I certainly was not ready to
deal with the consequences of such demands. And so I
steered clear of the text.

I know that Jesus does not mean that I should actually
hate my parents, or my wife or my children. His command
that I should love them, honour them, respect them, love
them as much as I love my own life, still stands. There is a
deeper meaning to this "hatred"; it is more than our human
definition of it as "utter resentment". It means that while
we love them we must realize that love for the Messiah,
obedience to the Messiah, comes before and above all. It is
to know that a time may come when all other obedience
must give way to that obedience, when all other commitments must give way to that ultimate commitment.
Nothing, not love of father, mother, wife or children,
brother or sister, or even one's own life, must then stand in
the way of that obedience.

You see, *that* is what makes it all so difficult. It is not easy
to stand in front of a government which represents an oppressive, inhuman power and say to it: "I must obey God
rather than you." But how infinitely more difficult it is to
look at the ones whom you love, whose love for you is at the

root of their concern for your safety, your wellbeing and your life, and to say to them: "I must obey God rather than you."

But this is precisely the consequence if we take these words seriously. That indeed is "the cost of discipleship". And we are not fully prepared for it, even though we may have had intellectual discussions, and we may have talked about it and seen it as a possibility for ourselves. It jolts us when we suddenly realize that we have no choice but to face the challenge.

I know, for I was in a plane somewhere between Nairobi and Johannesburg when I opened a newspaper and came across the account of the trial of the two Afrikaner Weerstandsbeweging[1] men in which, among other things, details of the plans to assassinate Bishop Desmond Tutu and myself were revealed. I shall not try to tell you how I felt. Nor shall I try to explain to you how I felt when our seven-year old daughter came home from school in tears and said: "Daddy, the children at school say that the white people are going to kill you." Many of you have read this too, and many of you were disturbed over it, in fact, so disturbed that my wife and I decided that I should speak about it. Hence this sermon.

We have received many signs of your concern, love and support during these days and we thank God, and you, for all of them. One really does not know what one would do without the warm, prayerful support of people who care.

We know that this is no idle threat. This movement has made clear its intention to "keep South Africa white", to rid it of the "dangerous, subversive elements" who are trying to change our society. They have openly declared their preparedness to use violence and, being white, they have the means to carry out these threats more effectively than anybody else. They are terrorists in every sense of the word. Yet they are allowed to go about and to operate by a government which bans Christian organizations, and Christian people who want to work for peaceful change in South Africa.

---

[1] Afrikaner Resistance Movement.

These people are dangerous. But they are not our deepest concern. Our concern is about a society in which violence has become endemic, in which racism has been given biblical sanction by churches and people who call themselves Christians — to such an extent that people will kill in order to preserve the privileges their white skin affords them in South Africa.

But why not? Their government has set them an example by the cold-blooded murder of harmless and unarmed children in the streets of Soweto in 1976 and in Cape Town in 1980, because these children's protest posed a threat to the white power structures in this country. Why should the Afrikaner Resistance Movement care about the life of a black person when racist laws, racist structures, racist attitudes emphasize in a thousand ways the sub-human status of black people in South Africa? Those of us who struggle for justice are called "communists" and Marxists and Leninists. We are labelled dangerous, as part of the "total onslaught of the forces of evil against South Africa". Small wonder then that there are these people who believe they will be doing God a favour by getting rid of those who dare call apartheid by the evil name it deserves.

I know of very few people who care more deeply for this country and its people than Desmond Tutu. I have seen him weep tears of anguish because of white people's unwillingness to understand, to respond humanly to black suffering and God's demands for justice. Very few have worked harder for reconciliation than he. And yet they want to kill him. As they killed Steve Biko, and Rick Turner, and James Gawe and so many others.

If they kill us, I want you to know: it is not because we have picked up a gun. It is not because we hated them, for even now I cannot bring myself to hate those misguided and violent men of the Afrikaner Resistance Movement whose only precious possession in life seems to be their white skin. If they kill us it is not because we have planned revolution. It will be because we have tried to stand up for justice, because we have tried to work for true peace. It is because we have refused to accept the cheap "reconciliation" which covers up evil, which denies justice, and which compromises the God-given dignity of black people. It will be because we love them so much that we refuse to allow them to continue to be our oppressors.

There are those of you who have asked me to reconsider my stand, to "take it easier", to tone it down a little bit. I know you did that because you care. Some of you argued forcefully with me, asking me to think of my wife and children. You did that out of your concern and love. Please do not think that I have not thought constantly about this. I too would like nothing better than to live with my family without fear, work with you as best as I can, experience the joys and pains of any normal father and husband. But not if that means I cannot do God's bidding in this struggle for justice and human dignity in this country. To struggle against apartheid is not simply to struggle *against* injustice and inhumanity. It is also to struggle *for* the integrity of the gospel of Jesus Christ. When I think of this, and when I think of the needless suffering of millions, caused by greed, political domination and racialism, I really have no choice. Besides, we have said so many times: it is not only the freedom of the oppressed that is at stake here but also the liberation of the oppressor. And we must all remember that there are some things so dear, some things so precious, some things so eternally true that they are worth dying for.

I have never spoken to you like this before. I hope that I shall never speak to you like this again. I must be honest with you: this is not bravado, I speak in fear and trepidation. I speak also in hope. Even if it is hoping against hope. At the same time I am absolutely certain: this is what I must do. I have a strange joy this morning, because I have discovered that I am no longer afraid, my life is in the hands of the God who is the Living One. I do not claim to understand everything that is happening to us, but I do know I want to do God's will.

I cannot but choose for justice, for the freedom of all the people of this land, oppressed and oppressor alike; I cannot but choose to fight for the human dignity of all God's children, to struggle for that day when "... there shall not be an infant that dies untimely; (my people) shall build houses and live in them, they will plant vineyards and eat their fruit. They will not build houses for others to live in or plant and not eat the fruit... Their labour shall not be in vain and the lives of their children shall not be destroyed..." (Isa. 65:20-24). That is what I must do — this is God's call and I must be obedient.

It was the old Herman Bavinck, that aristocrat of Dutch theologians, writing at a time in Europe very similar to ours in South Africa today, who reminded us that "a true theologian is one who, having everything against him, science and public opinion, state and church, and all things on earth, still clings to God and his Word, and in all things seeks God's honour and glory. Such honour is the ultimate goal and criterion of all things. It is God's unalienable right and his irretractable demand. To bring him that honour is our sacred duty and our highest privilege."

And Kaj Munk, that fearless father of Danish resistance against Hitler, prophet and pastor of the church, said in those turbulent days: "We (as ministers of the gospel) stand in the temple of the Holy God. All others have their obligations to this and to that, we alone have our obligations exclusive to the truth..."

And at another time: "But when justice or injustice is at stake, then we must never ask whether it is worth it, for then it is always the devil who wins. On these issues it is *always* worthwhile to fight." I hope fervently that something of this is being heard in what I am saying.

And I must admit that I have often felt like Jeremiah: a man who desires with all his heart a simple, peaceful life, but yet he is "doomed to strife". Many a time I vowed to be silent, but then "his Word was imprisoned in my body, like a fire blazing in my heart, and I was weary with holding it in and I cannot..." In some of my darkest moments of fear and despair I too cried out: "Lord, you have deceived, seduced me, and I let myself be seduced." I did *not* bargain for all this, I am *not* ready for all this, and I do not know how to answer the questions of my children or of my own heart.

But he who asks this of us is the One who became poor for our sake; He was forsaken by his father for our sake; he went through hell for our sake; he died and rose again, for us. His Spirit spoke to the prophets and still speaks to us so that even we, in our fear and uncertainty, may say once again with Jeremiah: "Lord, thou knowest...thy Word is joy and happiness to me, *for thou hast named me thine*."

7. Of grass and flowers and living words

A voice says: "Cry!"
And I said: "What shall I cry?"
All flesh is grass, and all its beauty
is like the flower of the field.
The grass withers, the flower fades,
when the breath of the LORD blows upon it;
surely the people is grass.
The grass withers, the flower fades;
but the word of our God endures for ever.

Isaiah 40:6-8

Chapter 40 of the Book of Isaiah marks the beginning of the second part of the book. It marks it so distinctly, so clearly, that most commentators speak of a "Second Isaiah".

Israel is still in exile. The darkness has not lifted, the light still refuses to shine. The suffering will not go away, and it seems as if all is lost. Too much suffering for too many years has extinguished the fires of hope in the eyes of too many. At this point in time, there is very little expectation in Israel; there is, rather, an acceptance of the situation — to the extent that many people have settled down, become used to their position of lowliness, of rejection and of oppression. Their concern is no longer liberation, it is simply survival.

They no longer have any belief in the far-off words of the prophets of old that Israel shall return to their own land. They no longer see in their mind's eye the beauty of Jerusalem, only the ruins which the holy city has become. And for many of them that symbolizes also the ruins of their own faith, their own hope, their own future. For is it not true that not only Israel's life, but also Israel's God is under siege? Israel had declared its faith in the one true God, Yahweh. The other gods did not count, they were non-entities. But as Israel's state and theology collapsed under the blows of this pagan power, were they not justified if they began to suspect that those gods were powerful after all? Had God finally, irrevocably, rejected Israel?

The endless questions find no answers and the cry "How long, LORD?" comes back as a mocking echo in the awful silence of God. It is only the words of Lamentations that they hear, words that etch out the pain and the hopelessness that the people feel:

> How lonely sits the city that was full of people;
> How like a widow she has become!
> She weeps bitterly in the night, tears on her cheeks;
> among all her lovers she has none to comfort her (1:1,2)

Freedom has fled for ever, it seems. Babylon is still as strong as ever, it seems. The people are helpless, and Yahweh is far away. It is no wonder that Israel groans: "My way is hid from the LORD, and my right is disregarded by my God..." (vs.27).

This scenario is not strange to people who have lived for so long under the yoke of oppression. It fits Lebanon today, or Afghanistan, or Namibia, or even South Africa. The Second Isaiah must speak against an incredible reality which seems to prove his every word a lie. How can one speak of the freedom that shall come, of a "new thing" that shall happen, of a God who will hear the people's cries, of hope that shall not have hoped in vain, when there is nothing to warrant these, and the enemy seems to be stronger than ever and the people's dreams dangle lifelessly at the end of Babylon's sword?

But the prophet says something more: "A voice says: Cry! What shall I cry? All flesh is grass, and all its beauty is like the flower of the field. The grass withers, the flower fades when the breath of the LORD blows upon it..."

We are used to hearing these words at funerals. And something of that is true. All human beings are like grass. We are so small, so vulnerable. We are born, we live, and we die; sometimes all to quickly, and too many die young, and too many die suddenly. Sometimes we live until we are seventy, or eighty or even ninety, and we look back and often we must ask: Have I really lived? It seems as if my life has sped away, it has slipped through my fingers like so much water. It may even be that I have been described as a success, I have done so much, and I should really be satisfied. But deep down I know that I have missed the things that really matter, that I may have been a failure. And so we hear these words and we say with the prophet:

Indeed it is true: all flesh is like grass, and its beauty is like the flower of the field. We are here today, gone tomorrow, blown away by the wind... and the beauty that we have shall wither and pass away when the breath of the Lord blows upon it.

It is true of all people. But I would like to suggest to you that this is especially true of those people who are the weak, the lowly, the poor and rejected, the meek and the oppressed, the voiceless and the defenceless. They, more than any other, know and experience this every single day of their lives. Their lives don't count, are of no worth in the eyes of those who are mighty and powerful and rich. Decisions are being made about them, and they have no say in them. They are being treated like so much dirt, and they have no defender. They are being pushed around the chessboard of life like so many pawns. All flesh is grass... it is true. But it is especially the weak and the poor, the defenceless and the lowly, who experience this.

We have seen it — in our history, in our own lifetime. In El Salvador, the soldiers of a Christian government, who must uphold the Christian values of that country, come into a little village where, it is alleged, the priest is an outspoken critic of the government and the people help the guerrillas. It is Sunday morning. The people are attending mass. The soldiers close the windows and doors from the outside and nail them fast with planks. Then they set fire to the building. Not one survives. Yes, it is true: all flesh is grass, and its beauty like the flower of the field. But no one knows this better than the weak, the lowly, the poor and the oppressed.

In Namibia the people of the small villages along the border are ravaged and terrorized by the South African Defence Force. An old man is caught, roasted alive on the coals, tortured for a few words of information — information that he did not even have. All flesh is grass, it withers, here today, gone tomorrow. And the weak, the poor, the lowly and the voiceless know it better than anyone else.

In a village in the Ciskei, Bishop Tutu visits people whose situation has become critical. They are dying of hunger. A little girl tells him that she eats when they can borrow food from the neighbours. "But if the neighbours don't have any?" he asks. Says the little girl: "Then we drink water to fill our stomachs..." And this in South Africa, one of the richest countries in the world, and certainly the wealthiest in Africa. Truly all flesh is grass, and the beauty of the flower withers, and the weak, the poor and the oppressed know it better than anyone else.

I will never forget the story told by Frieda Haddad from Lebanon, at the Sixth Assembly of the World Council of Churches in Vancouver. She told us about the tragic death of Dania, a little girl who died in an explosion caused by shelling from Israeli planes. Dania was a Muslim. A few weeks before it happened, she had accompanied a little friend from across the street to church. And she had asked the priest whether she could come with Rula to Sunday school. The priest didn't know what to advise her. But one day Dania came back, accompanied by her father who insisted that the two girls go to Sunday school together.

In Sunday school they talked about baptism. "But I am not baptized," said Dania. The teacher replied: "You do not need to be baptized by the priest in water. If we love Christ, then our love for him is our baptism." "I think", said Dania, "that when I get to know him better we will become good friends." The next day little Dania was blown to pieces. Indeed, all flesh is grass, and it withers like flowers of the field, and the poor, the weak, the voiceless, the little ones, know it better than anyone else.

But the prophet cries a second time. "All flesh is grass." This time, however, he adds something new: "The grass withers, the flower fades, *but the word of our God endures for ever.*"

In that situation, for the people of Israel, this is a new truth that they must come to understand. These words are not only applicable to the poor and the weak, the lowly and the rejected, to those who have no defender in the world. They are also applicable, in a special way, to the people who have put themselves upon a throne, who have made of themselves gods because they think that they are powerful. They rule the world and they rule the lives of the people of God with a ruthless hand. They put themselves in the place of God and they challenge the authority and the power of the Living One. They rape and murder and they call it justice. They kill and plunder and call it peace. Because they think themselves omnipotent, they take the words of the gospel and they overturn them to suit their own purposes. They take the life of the kingdom of God and make of it a mockery. So they talk about love and peace and justice and reconciliation, but all the while what we hear is blasphemy.

They can do it because they have power. And for a while they create the impression, and for a while we who live under their yoke believe them: they *are* omnipotent, they *are* all-powerful; our lives *are* in their hands and we *are* at their mercy. But Isaiah looks at them and says: All flesh is grass, the grass withers and the flower fades, but the word of our God endures for ever.

And it is true. Isaiah reminds his people of the God whom they worship:

> It is he who sits above the circle of the earth,
> and its inhabitants are like grasshoppers;
> (it is he) who stretches out the heavens like a curtain,
> and spreads them like a tent to dwell in;
> who brings princes to nought,
> and makes the rulers of the earth as nothing.
> Scarcely are they planted, scarcely sown,
> scarcely has their stem taken root in the earth,
> when he blows upon them and they wither,
> and the tempest (of his breath) carries them off
> like stubble.
> To whom then will you compare me,
> that I should be like him, says the Holy One...

(vs. 22-25)

It is indeed true. For there was once a Pharaoh who kept the people of Israel in bondage. Their subjection was complete; there seemed no end to the Pharaoh's power. He thought himself a god. We can still hear him, self-confident, arrogant, self-assured, seemingly secure in the knowledge of his own power: "Who is the LORD, that I should listen to his voice?" (Ex. 5:2).

But the God of Israel lifts his finger, and the plagues come, and the waters open, a path is carved through the sea

and through the wilderness, and the people of Israel live to
sing the song of liberation:

> I will sing to Yahweh, for he has triumphed gloriously;
> the horse and his rider he has thrown into the sea.
> Yahweh is my strength and my song,
> and he has become my liberation...
> Who is like thee, O LORD, among the gods?
> ...YAHWEH will reign for ever and ever... (Ex. 15)

So Israel came to understand that all flesh, even that of
the Pharaoh, is grass, it withers away when the breath of the
LORD blows upon it, but the Word of the Lord endures for
ever. The promises of God for his people, the promises of
love, of liberation, of humanity, of freedom, of wholeness,
of peace — those promises, that Word, will never die; it will
live for ever.

Nebuchadnezzar was the king who took Israel into exile.
Nebuchadnezzar was the most powerful ruler in the ancient
East at that time. Nebuchadnezzar was the king who caught
his god's (and his own) power and glory in a golden image
so that all the world should bow down before it, and pay
homage to him and acknowledge that he is a god. And yet
that same Nebuchadnezzar heard the voice of God in the
voices of the three young men who, out of obedience to
Yahweh, refused to bow down to the image.

And Israel returned from exile, and Jerusalem was re-
built, and out of the ashes and the ruins, out of the
hopelessness and despair rose the temple, the symbol of the
presence of God in the midst of God's people. Because it is
true: all flesh, even Nebuchadnezzar, is grass, but the word
of the Lord endures for ever.

Hitler came on the stage of history and was so sure that he
would initiate the kingdom of Aryan power and racial puri-
ty. And indeed, for a moment it seemed as if nothing could
check this man. For a moment it seemed as if his soldier's
boot would crush to earth all hope, all truth, all life in
Europe and elsewhere. And even as the guns of the allied
forces were heard outside Berlin, Dietrich Bonhoeffer died
on the gallows, and even as the moment of liberation came
for Denmark, little, weak Kaj Munk died at the hands of the

Gestapo. Because he could kill these prophets of God, snuff out their lives, and blow them out like a candle, for a moment Hitler thought, and many with him, that he would indeed rule for ever. But the truth was vindicated once again: all flesh is grass, even Hitler, but the word of the Lord will stand for ever.

Forty years later, Kaj Munk rises up in his country to become a symbol of hope, a symbol of defiance, a symbol of truth and of prophetic clarity. And even though Kaj Munk died in the fields of Jutland in Denmark forty years ago, his testimony, his witness, his words and his life, even his death, will stand as a sign of the kingdom of God, a sign of the power of this Word of our God that shall endure for ever.

Today in this country it seems as if the power of this government is unassailable, and their might is unchallengeable. Indeed, there are those who think that they can place themselves on the throne of the Almighty and that they can take it upon themselves to pass judgment on the church of Jesus Christ because it dares stand up for justice and peace. Because they have power they think they can control the life of the church, they can define for the church what our ministry ought to be, what our witness ought to be; they can decide for us how we should preach the Word of God. They do appear invincible now, and they smile triumphantly because they have proved that peace comes out of the barrel of a gun, and the world applauds them while the innocent in this land continue to die. But all flesh is grass, and withers like the flower of the field. And they shall know it, they shall experience it, and the world shall see it, for the mouth of the Lord has spoken. And the Word of the Lord endures for ever.

For that Word is a word of love, a word of justice, a word of forgiveness, a word of mercy and of everlasting truth. It is a word of power. As surely as the words of the prophets live today; as surely as the words of the martyrs of the church live today; as surely as the words of Dietrich Bonhoeffer, Kaj Munk and Martin Luther King live today; so the words and the life and the witness of the South African Council of Churches shall live, shall be remembered and honoured, shall inspire us long after the world would have forgotten that there was a time when in this country apartheid ruled supreme.

And so let us not think, because of our own despair of the moment, because of the darkness that envelops us, because the contours of the kingdom of God appear distorted and unclear when seen through the veil of suffering and pain and anger — let us not think that God has forgotten the lot of the people in this land. Even though it may seem so for the moment, it is not true. For those who think that they rule the world are flesh, they are like the flowers of the field. The grass withers, and the flower fades, but the word of our God will stand for ever.

Let us therefore not falter in our obedience to this God, let us remain faithful to him and to his promises. Let us work for, and let us believe in humanity, that it shall become a sign of the kingdom of God. Let us work for, and believe in justice, that it shall become a sign of the kingdom of God. Let us work for, and believe in love, that it shall become a sign of the kingdom of God. Let us work for, and believe in true peace and reconciliation, that it shall become a sign of the kingdom of God. Let us believe in the power of God, that it shall become real, and that it shall overturn even our history and hasten that day when "every valley shall be exalted and every mountain and hill made low; the rough places shall be made plains. And the glory of the LORD shall be revealed and all flesh shall see it together" (vs. 4,5).

For it is true. The grass withers — even us; the flower fades — even us; but the Word of our God endures for ever.

8. A letter to the South African Minister of Justice

The Honourable A. Schlebusch
Minister of Justice, Union Building
Pretoria 0002   24 August 1979

Dear Mr Minister,

A short while ago you thought it right to address sharply the South African Council of Churches as well as church leaders, over radio and television and in the press, in connection with the SACC resolution on civil disobedience. Although the decision was not taken as a direct result of my address at the meeting, I had expressed my point of view openly on that occasion and I was one of the people who supported the SACC resolution.

You are Minister of Justice and in this capacity you have issued your serious warning. I take your words seriously. Hence my reaction, which I express with all respect, and which you must read particularly as a personal declaration of faith.

Your warning has become almost customary in South Africa. In it you continually point out to pastors and churches that they must keep themselves "out of politics" and confine themselves to their "proper" task: the preaching of the gospel.

Here already an extremely important question emerges: what is the gospel of Jesus Christ which the churches have been called to preach? Surely it is the message of the salvation which God offers to all people through Jesus Christ. It is the proclamation of the kingdom, and of the lordship of Christ. But this salvation is the making whole of the *whole person*. It is not meant for one's "inner life", or soul, only. It is meant for one's whole human existence. This Jesus who is proclaimed by the church was surely not only a spiritual being with spiritual qualities estranged from the reality of our human existence. No, he is the Word become flesh, who took on complete human form, and his message of liberation is meant for the total person in his or her *full humanity*.

Besides, the fact that the term *kingdom* is so politically loaded must already say a great deal to us. For example, the fact that reformed Christians have rightly professed with conviction throughout the centuries that the lordship of Christ applies to *all* spheres of our lives — the political, social and economic spheres also. The Lord rules over all these, and the church and the Christian proclaim God's sovereignty in all these spheres. Surely it is a holy duty and the calling of every Christian to participate in political life so that there also God's law and justice may prevail, and there also obedience to God and God's Word can be shown.

The Dutch Reformed Church professes this in its report *Ras, Volk en Nasie in die lig van die Heilige Skrif* ("Race, People and Nation in the Light of the Holy Gospel"). The report states plainly that the church in its proclamation must appeal to its members to apply the principles of the kingdom of God in the social and political sphere. When the Word of God demands it, the church must fulfill its prophetic function with regard to the state in spite of popular opinion. The witness of the church with regard to the government is a part of its essential being, says the report. The Dutch Reformed Church professes this because it wants to be Reformed. Why then is this profession, and participation, not granted to other Christians (and other Reformed Christians)?

There is still another problem.

Through its spokespeople your government has often warned that clergy "must keep out of politics". Yet at the same time it is your own colleagues in the cabinet who want to involve those of us who serve in the churches in political dialogue!

The only conclusion which I can come to is that you do not object in principle to the participation of clergy in politics — as long as it happens on your terms. This seems to me to be a standpoint which is neither tenable nor honest. In addition, are you not denying your own history by holding on to this view? Did not Afrikaner clergy speak as leaders of their people, and did they not inspire their people in their struggle? Did not the church of the Afrikaner, even in the Anglo-Boer War, stand right in the middle of the struggle? Why do you today reject with a sort of political pietism that which yesterday and the day before you embraced with thankfulness to God?

But, Mr Minister, there is something more in your warning. It has to do with the exceptionally difficult and sensitive issue of a Christian's obedience to the government.

It is important that you understand clearly that I made my call for civil disobedience as a *Christian* to other *Christians*.

It surprises me that some people see in this a call for violence. It is precisely an alternative to violence! I look to this alternative because I still do not believe that the way of violence is the proper way.

Or is it the fear that when Christians "obey God more than men", the whole idolized nature of this state will be exposed? Surely the state in which Christ reigns (as you claim he does) shouldn't have to be afraid of this? In addition, I am of the opinion that I have done nothing more than to place myself squarely within the Reformed tradition.

Essential to all of this is the following:

It is my conviction that, for a Christian, obedience to the state or any authority is always linked to the obedience to God. That is to say, obedience to human institutions is always relative. The human institutions can never have the same authority as God, and human laws must always be subordinate to the Word of God. This is how the Christian understands it. Since God does not expect blind obedience from God's children, Christians cannot even think of giving unconditional obedience to a worldly sovereignty.

Over the years it has become clear to me that your government expects precisely that sort of unconditional, blind obedience. I want to be honest with you: this I cannot give you. The believer in Christ has not only the right, but also the responsibility, to be more obedient to God and God's law than to the government, should the government deviate from God's law.

Through the years, nearly all the large Christian churches in South Africa have condemned the policy of your government as sinful and wrong. My own church, the D.R. Mission Church, last year condemned the policy of this government as being "in conflict with the gospel of Jesus Christ, a policy which cannot stand up to the demands of the gospel". I heartily endorse this statement of my church. Your policy is unjust, it denies people their basic human rights, and it undermines their humanity. Too many of the laws which you make are in conflict with the Word of God.

Your policy and its execution are a tremendous obstacle for reconciliation between the people of South Africa. Some of the laws are more hurtful than others and have been condemned especially by the churches. Now the churches have reached a point where we say: If we condemn laws on the grounds of God's Word, how can we then obey those very same laws?

In my view, Christians in South Africa today do not stand alone in this decision. The scriptures know of disobedience to powers when these powers disregarded the Word of the Living God.

Daniel's three friends refused to obey the king's law when they refused to bow down before the graven image of Nebuchadnezzar (Dan. 3:17-18). They regarded the king's laws as being in conflict with the instructions of their God.

Peter's refusal to obey the Sanhedrin's command not to witness about Jesus any more is the classic example of disobedience to a worldly authority. To this day his answer resounds in the church of Christ: "We must obey God rather than men" (Acts 5:29).

This, despite the fact that in the case of Peter and John the Sanhedrin was the highest authority, not only in religious matters but in everything which did not lie directly under the jurisdiction of the Roman procurator.

There are still other examples. Paul displayed nothing of a servile obedience when the magistrate at Philippi wanted to release him from prison after confining him unlawfully (without a trial!). "They gave us a public flogging, though we are Roman citizens and have not been found guilty; they threw us into prison, and are they now to smuggle us out privately? No indeed!" (Acts 16:37).

In the case of Paul, the judges were the highest officials in the Roman colony of Philippi. For both Peter and Paul it was clear that occasions could arise when the only way out would be disobedience to the unjust authority. Still more of these examples. Luke 23:6-12, Mark 15:1-5 and John 18:8-11 teach us that Jesus did not always demonstrate obedience to state authority. Before Herod, he refused to say a word: "He answered him without a word." Also before Pilate, according to Mark, Jesus gave no answer, either to the questions of Pilate, or to the charges of the high priest.

John tells us that Jesus reminded Pilate of something of which every worldly bearer of authority must be reminded: "You would have no authority at all over me if it had not been granted you from above; and therefore the deeper guilt lies with the man who handed me over to you" (John 19:11).

I am not saying that these actions of Jesus or Peter and Paul "prove" that a revolutionary overthrow of the state can be justified. That is a completely different issue. I am saying here that blind obedience to civil authorities is alien to the Bible and that, for a Christian, loyalty and obedience is first and foremost to God.

May I point out, in parenthesis, that the issue on which everything hinges and which South Africa has to learn is certainly not servile submissiveness of citizens to the state but *co-responsibility* for the affairs of state. And it is precisely this which the policy of your government denies millions of citizens.

This is not the place to present a full explanation on Romans 13. However, I would point out that the first verse of Romans 13, which is often taken as a blank legitimization of state interference, is in fact a very serious point of criticism. A government yields authority because (and *as long as*) it reflects the authority of God: liberating, creative, serving. Thus Paul can refer to a government as a *servant of God* "for your good". Thus, throughout the years, it has been taken for granted in the Reformed thinking that a government wields authority for as long as there is evidence that it is accepting responsibility for law and for justice. Where justice is lacking, however, the government's authority is no longer derived from God but is in conflict with God. In such a case, resistance against such a government is justified and becomes a duty.

Even Augustine, one of the fathers of the church who was particularly concerned about protecting the state and defended state authority with extraordinary energy, had this to say: "Justice is the only thing that can give a worldly power worth. What is a worldly government if justice is lacking? It is none other than a bunch of plunderers."

Calvin also saw this and he held that "worldly princes" lose all their power when they rise up against God; he stated clearly that Christians should resist such a power rather than obey it.

The point is of course to decide when a government collides with the demands of God's Word. In this the church should be led by the Word itself through the justice of the kingdom of God, and also by the actual experience of people. Because it is in the concrete situation of people that the Word shows itself alive and more powerful, and sharper than any two-edged sword.

In this the church should find its criteria; not from those who are favoured by the laws, but rather from those who are hurt by these laws, hurt at their deepest level of being; those who have no voice, the voteless, the vulnerable ones; the oppressed, the "least of these my brethren".

And with the least of the brethren in our country, your government and your policy stand condemned. I don't have to repeat the accusations again. I just want to draw your attention to the fact.

The sufferings of men, women and children, the wounds caused by your policy through the years can never be compensated for by "concessions". The superficial adjustments already made by your government do not touch the root of the matter. It is as one of your own colleagues has said: "The fact that a black man carries a springbok emblem doesn't give him political rights." Indeed. We can add: it doesn't give him his God-given humanity either.

It is because of your policy that so many churches and so many Christians find themselves against you. In this we really have no choice, because the church of Christ in South Africa must obey God more than people. I plead with you: stop your disastrous policy before it's too late.

May I end with a personal word? I am not writing this letter in order to prove myself brave or because of arrogance. I must honestly confess that I am afraid of you. You are the Minister of Justice. You have at your disposal powers which only a fool would underestimate. The victims of this power are sown across the path of South Africa's past and recent history.

I, like any other South African, want to live a normal life with my wife and children. I want to serve the church without fear. I want a country where freedom is seen as the right of every citizen and not as a gift from the government. I want, along with millions of other people, to have co-responsibility in my native country, with everything you grant yourself and your children. I also want peace, but real peace. Not the fearful silence which we have now, but that peace which is the fruit of active justice for all.

But my wish for a "normal life" must not undermine the service I am called to. That would be intolerable. And my service is also towards you. That is why I write this letter. I shall stand guilty before God if I do not witness against this government.

I think the time has come for your government to make a choice between the servant of God in Romans 13 and the demon in Revelations 13. And unless the right choice becomes evident though a whole-hearted and fundamental change of your policy, Christians in South Africa will have to continue to resist you as we would the beast of Revelations 13.

I am aware that resistance against a government is not an easy decision to make. That is why the synod of the Dutch Reformed Mission Church made it so clear last year: "If a Christian finds himself bound by his conscience to follow the way of criticism which brings himself into conflict with the state, then he should obey God more than men. In this case, however, he must be prepared to accept suffering in the spirit of Christ and his apostles."

Once again, this is not a matter of being brave. Rather I would like to use the occasion seriously to urge you to realize that peace and salvation and a happy future for South Africa do not lie in more "security laws" or in more threats or in an ever-growing defence budget. Rather they lie in the pursuit of justice for all South Africa's children...

I am using this letter as an open witness and thus will make it available to the press.

I thank you for giving me your time. May God give you wisdom in all things.

Yours sincerely,

Dr A.A. Boesak